IMAGES
of America

FILIPINOS IN VALLEJO

IMAGES
of America

FILIPINOS
IN VALLEJO

Mel Orpilla

ARCADIA
PUBLISHING

Published by Arcadia Publishing
Charleston, South Carolina

Library of Congress Catalog Card Number: 2004117441

For all general information contact Arcadia Publishing at:
Telephone 843-853-2070
Fax 843-853-0044
E-mail sales@arcadiapublishing.com
For customer service and orders:
Toll-Free 1-888-313-2665

Visit us on the Internet at www.arcadiapublishing.com

The author, Mel Orpilla, wears his favorite sailor suit in this photo from 1964. (Courtesy of Orpilla family.)

CONTENTS

Dedicated to my parents
Nazario and Ofelia Orpilla

And in loving memory of
Modesto and Aurelia Orpilla
Clemente and Manuela Orpilla
Leon and Connie Orpilla
Grandma Mary Hullana

ACKNOWLEDGMENTS

The making of this book would not have been possible without the help of some very important people in my life. My wife, Belle, helped with the editing of the captions and text, but more importantly supported me through this endeavor. My lifelong friend, Lionel Galiste, helped me scour the *Vallejo Times-Herald* photo files for images of Filipinos. He also brought some wonderful photos from his own family's collections. Thanks also to Ted Volmer, editor of the *Vallejo Times-Herald*, who gave Lionel and me free rein of the photo archives. Kudos to Jim Kern, executive director of the Vallejo Naval and Historical Museum, who also opened the museum's archives. Jim also provided me with helpful hints and guidance throughout this project as the author of a previous Arcadia book.

I want to thank all the individuals and organizations that contributed photos from their albums and collections to this book. Some had to dig in boxes that had not been opened for decades. Others had story upon story to tell about their parents or of "growing up Pinoy" in Vallejo. Most of all, we enjoyed reminiscing about the "old days" when life was simpler, or so it seemed. Contributors include my parents, Ofelia and Nazario Orpilla, Nieves Fernandez, Lionel Galiste, Fellowship United Methodist Church, Filipino-American Catholic Club, Councilman Pete Rey, Filipino-American National Historical Society–Vallejo Chapter, Ed Dumaguin, Marcella Thurmon, Simon Vargas, Charles Castillo, Jaime Juanillo, Dan Tiburcio, Venus Rumbaoa, Jose Bautista, Julie Dizon, Rena Fulgencio, Adela Genio Pascual and Alberto Pascual, Florie and Denny Barnett, Emily Calica, Filipino-American Social Services, Alice Realiza, Pastor Rey Bernardes, Zacarias Cordero, Pat Bacol Mendoza, Mare Island Historic Park Foundation's Peggy O'Drain, Emil Bautista, and Joyce Scharf.

In 1991, along with a group interested in Vallejo's Filipino history, I founded the Filipino-American National Historical Society–Vallejo Chapter (FANHS). Since then, some of those original members have passed on. It is my hope that their legacy will live on through the images in this book. They include Helen Marquez, Joe Fortes, Cesar Alemania, Lucille Adoptante, and Evelyn Rillera. Another member I wish to acknowledge is the late Helen Toribio of the East Bay Chapter, who influenced so many budding activists, historians, students, and writers. May they and all the departed Filipinos mentioned in this book rest in peace with the knowledge that their stories are finally being told.

INTRODUCTION

Twenty years ago, in an Ethnic Studies class taught by Wayne Maeda at California State University, Sacramento, I discovered that Filipinos did indeed have a history in America. It was a revelation to me to know that my father, who came to America in 1926, experienced the most tragic era in Filipino-American history when he and many others faced discrimination and oppression upon arriving in this country. Up until that time, I took his experience and those of the "Manongs," (Filipino old-timers) for granted. More importantly, learning about Filipino-American history strengthened my connections to my family, community, and Filipino roots.

As a photographer, I have taken thousands of rolls of film. As a photo collector, I have almost as many images in my vast collection depicting Filipinos in America. I knew that eventually I would need to compile them into a book. For years people had been encouraging me to write a book about Filipino-American history. Finally that time has come.

It was important for me to feature Vallejo's Filipino history because there is almost no mention of it in any textbook. Having been born and raised in Vallejo, I knew that a Filipino community had thrived there since almost the turn of the last century. My collections started with my father's photos taken before and after World War II. The images depicted a vibrant city, with handsome "Pinoy" (Filipino) bachelors who were planting the seeds of a strong cultural, economic, and political community.

Throughout the pages of this book are images of children, teenagers, young families, and parties. The Filipino community is family-oriented; however, Filipinos have large extended families that may or may not be related by blood. The pages of this book also depict Filipinos assimilating or trying to assimilate into the broader community. Sometimes they were successful, as in the case of Lucy Dizon, and sometimes they were not, such as the Filipino Brownie troop, formed because little Filipina girls were not allowed to join "white" Brownie troops.

In any case, Filipinos have had a presence in Vallejo since right after the Spanish-American War. They established a Manilatown on lower Georgia Street with restaurants, bars, barbershops, pool halls, and other gathering spots. Filipinos were stationed at Mare Island Naval Shipyard during and after World War II and brought their families with them to Vallejo. In 1965, relaxed immigration laws led to an explosion in the Filipino population with professionals, medical personnel, and Navy men making Vallejo their permanent home in America. At the time this book was written, the Filipino population in Vallejo accounted for about a quarter of the overall population, or approximately 25,000 Filipinos.

Filipinos in Vallejo is about family, community, and home. The images represent the lives of Vallejo's pioneer Filipino families and the new generation of Filipinos who call Vallejo home today. To them and their ancestors still living in Vallejo, this book is a testament to the Filipino community's "bamboo" spirit—of taking root, spreading out, and of bending in the wind but never breaking.

One

BACHELOR SOCIETY

Thousands of single Filipino men immigrated to America between 1906 and 1934. They came looking for work, adventure, and a new life in America. Because the Philippines were an American territory, Filipinos were classified as "American Nationals" and were allowed to immigrate without restrictions. Many ended up in Vallejo, where good-paying jobs at Mare Island were plentiful. Pictured c. 1953, the "Big Five" from South Vallejo are, from left to right, Roy Marinas, Zacarias Cordero, Ted Soriano, Maurice Ancheta, and George Banez. (Courtesy of Zacarias Cordero.)

Like many Filipino bachelors, Daniel Jose Tiburcio came to America in 1927. He began work at the Mare Island Naval Shipyard before World War II, then joined the U.S. Army, serving in the historic First Filipino Battalion. Mare Island was the economic magnet that attracted Filipino workers to Vallejo. Mare Island provided Filipinos with good-paying, steady employment with paid vacations, sick leave, and health benefits. (Courtesy of Daniel Tiburcio.)

Bernardo Bolao Bacol (middle) poses c. 1920 with some of his bachelor friends. He worked at Mare Island Naval Shipyard as a laborer for 32 years before retiring from Shop 72 in 1979. (Courtesy of Pat Bacol Mendoza.)

Many bachelor Filipinos lived in boardinghouses run by other Filipinos. Mary Hullana operated a boardinghouse at 46 Carolina Street. Pictured in this c. 1949 photo outside the boardinghouse, from left to right, are Nazario Orpilla, Mary Hullana, and Bernard Hullana. The Filipino male-to-female ratio in America during this time period was approximately 14:1. (Courtesy of Nazario Orpilla.)

Box dances and queen contests were some of the favorite weekend activities for the single men looking to meet and socialize with Filipinas, who were a rare sight in the early days. Here, Juan Sarmiento is standing in the middle with Adele Bautista on his right, c. 1950. (Courtesy of Nazario Orpilla.)

Members of the Legionarios del Trabajo in America Vallejo Lodge pose for a *c.* 1955 group photo at the Veterans Memorial Building. The fraternity was established in America in 1924 and provided a support network and opportunities to foster leadership and community development skills. Lodges were established from San Diego to Seattle. (Courtesy of Nazario Orpilla.)

Nazario Orpilla came to America in 1926 as a 20 year old with a sixth-grade education. This was typical of the Filipinos arriving in America. They could read, write, and speak English due to the imposition of the American educational system in the Philippines in 1901. Nazario is wearing his Legionarios hat in this photo, which was taken when he first joined in 1941. (Courtesy of Nazario Orpilla.)

In this *c.* 1949 photo, Hullana boardinghouse owner Mary Hullana and Nazario Orpilla sit in a car in front of the house on Carolina Street. "Grandma Mary" was a well-known matron of the Filipino community who provided housing to dozens of single Filipino men after the war. (Courtesy of Nazario Orpilla.)

Most Filipino boardinghouses, like this one in downtown Vallejo, were established in turn-of-the-century Victorians. Other Filipino-owned boardinghouses included those operated by the Pabrua, Argonza, and Aliga families. (Courtesy of Julie Dizon.)

The 1941 Filipino Community of Solano County Ping Pong Tournament was held downstairs in Louis Lopez's business on Georgia Street. Lopez was one of the most successful Filipino businessmen and community leaders. (Courtesy of the Galiste family.)

Pictured here c. 1940, Lorenzo Asera first arrived in Mankas Corner in Solano County in 1920, then moved to Vallejo in 1927 after getting a job as a helper at Mare Island Naval Shipyard. He was a member of the Caballeros Dimas Alang, Bonifacio Lodge fraternity. (Courtesy of Larry Asera.)

Boxing was a favorite pastime for many Filipino bachelors. Filipino boxers, especially in the lightweight ranks, dominated the boxing world. Sonny Hatsme was the 1939 Midwest Flyweight Champion and a contender for the World's Flyweight Boxing title. (Courtesy of the Vallejo Naval and Historical Museum.)

Pictured here around 1939, Lorenzo Calica played his beloved saxophone until he was 91 years old. He played in many bands, including the much-heralded Manila Serenaders, and traveled throughout the United States. He also played in the U.S. Army's Filipino Infantry Band. (Courtesy of Emily Calica.)

Nazario Orpilla poses *c.* 1955 in Legionarios Del Trabajo official regalia. (Courtesy of Nazario Orpilla.)

The Legionarios Del Trabajo are shown here *c.* 1955. (Courtesy of Nazario Orpilla.)

Filipino houseboys were favored by Hollywood movie stars as well as the rich. Lorenzo Dizon, posing in his chauffeur uniform in Hollywood, was actress Mary Pickford's driver in the 1930s. Since Filipinos spoke English fluently due to the American public school system in the Philippines, they made good houseboys. (Courtesy of Julie Dizon.)

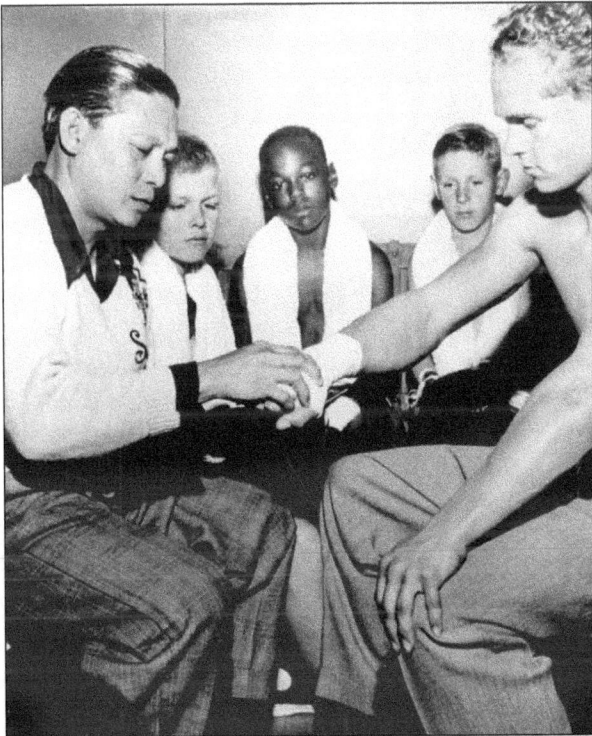

In this c. 1952 photo, Sonny Hatsme, volunteer trainer of the Carquinez Heights Boxing Squad, wraps bandages on 1950 champion Jim Peck while interested juniors look on. (Courtesy of the Vallejo Naval and Historical Museum.)

17

Zacarias Cordero, last of the South Vallejo "Big Five" bachelors, is shown in 1999 at his South Vallejo home on Sheridan Street. (Courtesy of Mel Orpilla.)

The Legionarios del Trabajo was a Filipino fraternal organization, and Vallejo's lodge still meets after 60 years. Pictured c. 1950, from left to right, are (front row) ? Banayat, Mary Hullana, and unidentified; (back row) Bernard Hullana and Nazario Orpilla. (Courtesy of Nazario Orpilla.)

Two

FAMILY LIFE

Charlita Balolong's baptism at the apartment of Frank and Salud Verano on Virginia Street in downtown Vallejo took place c. 1949. Early Filipinos came from various regions in the Philippines, including Ilocos, La Union, Pangasinan, Bohol, and other Visayan Islands. This is a group of Boholanans from the island of Bohol in the Philippines. (Courtesy of the Galiste family.)

The Philippine-American War was a catalyst for Filipinos coming to Vallejo. Many of the ships used in battle and to transport troops departed from and returned to Mare Island. Maria Martinez, pictured here c. 1915, married soldier George Washington Carter in the Philippines and moved to Vallejo in 1912 after crocodiles kept eating the pigs they were raising on their pig farm. (Courtesy of Alice Realiza.)

One of the first Filipino natives in Vallejo was Alice Carter, who was born at the family home at 233 Florida Street to Maria Martinez Carter and George Washington Carter. She poses with her daughter Caroline in this 1936 photo. (Courtesy of Alice Realiza.)

Ignacio and Placida Vargas gathered their family together for this *c.* 1951 group photo. Seated, from left to right, are (front row) children Carol and Simon; (back row) Billy, Joe, Helen, Rey, and Thelma. The family lived on Ohio Street. (Courtesy of Simon Vargas.)

Daniel Tiburcio and sons Daniel and Robert are shown *c.* 1948 at Chabot Acres housing project, government housing set up for Mare Island Naval Shipyard employees, off Mini Drive and Everest Street. (Courtesy of Daniel Tiburcio.)

Most Filipino families lived downtown and in the St. Vincent's Hill neighborhood. Basilia Largo lived at the corner of Marin and York Streets. Pictured c. 1952 on the steps, from top to bottom, are Basilia Largo, Tonia Galiste, Julito Balolong, Sergia Balulong, and Charlita Bululong. (Courtesy of the Galiste family.)

The Calica family lived on Branciforte Street in the St. Vincent's Hill neighborhood. Pictured c. 1957 are parents Lorenzo and Mercedes, with children Emily and Arlene. (Courtesy of Emily Calica.)

Filipinos love to have parties. Weddings, religious holidays, birthdays, and baptisms were always occasions to celebrate. This is Esther Banez (center) at her baby shower in 1956. (Courtesy of the Galiste family.)

Lorenzo and Rufina Asera pose c.1949 with their young cousin and grandson, Larry Asera, in front of their 1820 Ohio Street home. (Courtesy of Larry Asera.)

Blue Rock Springs Park in East Vallejo was a popular place for community picnics. Originally home to an exclusive hot springs resort, around 1960 it was turned into a public park for all to enjoy. (Courtesy of Nazario Orpilla.)

In this *c.* 1952 photo taken at the Vallejo waterfront (with St. Vincent's Hill in the background), Julito Balolong holds his daughter Charlita while son Julito Jr. rides. (Courtesy of the Galiste family.)

Interracial marriages were common in Vallejo, in spite of laws that barred Filipinos and whites from getting married in California. Marcelo Teofilo and his wife, Grace, hold Marcella, six months old, and Gary, three years old, outside their home at the Carquinez Heights housing project, c.1946. (Courtesy of Marcella Thurmon.)

After the war, many Filipinos joined the U.S. Navy at Sangley Point in the Philippines. Some were stationed at Mare Island Naval Shipyard and made Vallejo their home. In this c. 1963 photo, Adela Genio Pascual poses with her children Linda, Theresa, and Edgar, in the Larwin Plaza Shopping Center, which is now called Vallejo Plaza. The car is a 1960 Chevy Impala. (Courtesy of the Pascual family.)

Mrs. Maxine "Manang Maming" Llaguno pushes her son Vincent near the Vallejo waterfront with St. Vincent's Hill in the distance, c. 1939. The little girl in the background is Pat Bacol. (Courtesy of Pat Bacol Mendoza.)

Pictured at this Christmas Party in Vallejo in 1951, from left to right, are (front row) Lorenzo Calica, Esparanza Calica, unidentified, Mauricio Calica, Delfin Calica, and unidentified; (back row) Jack Jacildo, Mercedes Calica, Arleen Calica (baby), Luisa Evangelista, and Claudio Evangelista (holding Pricilla). (Courtesy of Emily Calica.)

Gloria Geray, a second-generation Filipina, married Henry Asera, son of Lorenzo and Rufina Asera. She is seen here with her sons, Daniel and Larry, in their Carquinez Heights home in 1954. Larry would grow up to become Vallejo's first Filipino city councilman. (Courtesy of Larry Asera.)

The Bacol family lived in an apartment at the corner of Santa Clara and Georgia Streets. Pictured c. 1938, from left to right, are Esperanza Bacol ("Peping"), Rose Castaneda, her daughter Rose Castaneda ("Young Rose"), Dorie Ridola, Juanita Bacol at age four, Faustino Bacus, and Pat Bacol. (Courtesy of Pat Bacol Mendoza.)

27

Frank Fabillaran, who came to America in 1924, is shown here with his wife, Marcy, holding their son David at Blue Rock Springs Park, *c.* 1960. At that time, Blue Rock Springs had a miniature train that ran around the park. Notice the train tunnel in the background. (Courtesy of Marcella Thurmon.)

An early group photo in Vallejo shows Venancio Llaguno (back row, far right) *c.* 1932. He is the father of Vincent, Venie, Verna, and Victor Llaguno. (Courtesy of Pat Bacol Mendoza.)

The Bacol family celebrate Pat's fourth birthday on the roof of their home at the corner of Georgia and Santa Clara Streets, with the Hotel Georgian in the background. Pictured, from left to right, are Pat Bacol, Bernardo Bacol, Juanita Bacol, Angelina Guilling, Vincent Llaguno, George Ridola, Florence Morris, Joey Reyes, Robert Ridola, Fay Reyes, Albert Reyes, Lily Reyes, Ester Reyes, Dodong Reyes, and Leo Reyes. (Courtesy of Pat Bacol Mendoza.)

Rosie Fabillaran and Danny Tobon hold Marcella Teofilo during her baptism at St. Vincent's Church, c. 1946. (Courtesy of Marcella Thurmon.)

This gathering at Mary Hullana's home at 46 Capital Street was held around 1950. Mary Hullana is at the far right. The children in the front row include Patricia and Virginia Orpilla and Jimmy Hullana. (Courtesy of Nazario Orpilla.)

The Pascual family lived at 217 Gardner Street in Federal Terrace Navy Housing, where they lived rent-free because their father, Alberto, was in the Navy. This photo was taken in December 1963 after the family had attended church wearing their Sunday best. (Courtesy of the Pascual family.)

This gathering, which took place c. 1950, included the Florendo, Ancheta, Orpilla, Fusilero, Bambao, and Hullana families. (Courtesy of Nazario Orpilla.)

South Vallejo was another neighborhood where Filipinos settled after World War II. Eva Rumbaoa, Ernesto Visaya, Florie Rumbaoa, and Rudy Rumbaoa pose in front of their home at 1032 Fifth Street, c. 1960.

The Pete and Beaula Galope family gather with friends outside their Alameda Street home, c. 1947. (Courtesy of the Galiste family.)

Many Filipinos who served the United States during World War II went back to the Philippines to marry. Nazario Orpilla met Ofelia through a friend in Vallejo, who happened to be her cousin. They corresponded over a year and got married in 1959. (Courtesy of Nazario Orpilla.)

Manuela Orpilla holds her daughter Pat outside of their home at the Carquinez Heights housing project, c. 1948. Standing next to them are her other two children, Virginia and Cristen. (Courtesy of Virginia Orpilla.)

Families that lived in the Federal Terrace housing project sent their children to Federal Terrace Elementary School. Here Theresa, Steve, and Alberto Pascual stand in front of the school in 1964. (Courtesy of the Pascual family.)

The baptism of Ricky Orpilla took place *c.* 1956 at St. Vincent's Church. Standing, from left to right, are Aurelia and Modesto Orpilla, Tirso Estepa, and unidentified. (Courtesy of Nazario Orpilla.)

Mollie Tiburcio and Lela LaCosta are shown here at the Chabot Acres housing project, c. 1945. Mollie performed Hawaiian dances at local parties and in the Delta. Lela's husband was a member of a Hawaiian band. (Courtesy of Daniel Tiburcio.)

This family photo shows Clemente Orpilla with his wife, Manuela, wearing a traditional Philippine butterfly dress, and their children, Virginia (on her father's lap) and Cristen, c. 1948. (Courtesy of Nazario Orpilla.)

Modesto Orpilla holds his son Ricky in this c. 1948 photo. Standing next to him are Mary Hullana and an unidentified man. The two children in the front are Virginia and Cristen Orpilla. (Courtesy of Nazario Orpilla.)

Marcelo Teofilo met his wife, Grace, on Mare Island. Here they are in front of their home at the Carquinez Heights housing project, c. 1946. Grace later worked at the Sears store in downtown Vallejo. (Courtesy of Marcella Thurmon.)

Three

BUILDING A COMMUNITY

As the Filipino community in Vallejo grew, they needed a place of their own to hold meetings and parties. This is the original site of the Filipino Community Center, at the corner of Grant and Cherry Streets in South Vallejo. Today it is located on the 800 block of Sonoma Boulevard. Among those shown in the photo are Librado Largo (fourth from left), Ben Mariano (second from right), and Feliciano Munar (far right). (Courtesy of Filipino-American National Historical Society–Vallejo Chapter.)

The founders of the Sekder Day Pangasinan organization, from left to right, included (front row) Bernardino Aquino, Carmen Valerio, Eustaquio Valerio, Leona Aquino, and Vitaliano Valerio; (back row) Tranquilino Aquino, Gregorio Damacion, Johnny Gaspar, Salvador Bautista, Catalino Aquino, and Eddie Aquino. This photo was taken c. 1955. (Courtesy of Jose Bautista.)

Jose Quiaoit works his plot at the Vallejo Community Garden at 240 Rogers Street in 1981. Mr. Quiaoit was a farm laborer before coming to Vallejo and enjoyed gardening. (Courtesy of Vallejo Times-Herald.)

To serve the needs of the Filipino community, numerous markets selling food items from the Philippines opened for business. One of the largest was the Philippine Grocery on Sonoma Boulevard. Manager Linda Gurion straightens the banana display at her store in 1981. (Courtesy of *Vallejo Times-Herald.*)

The Legionarios del Trabajo held many dinner dances at Casa de Vallejo's ballroom. Pictured c.1958, from left to right, are (front row) Mary Hullana, Julie Dizon, Adele Madayag, Alice Garcillano, and Camilla ?; (back row) Bernard Hullana, Nazario Orpilla, Pete Bambao, Mike Dilanilla, and unidentified. (Courtesy of Julie Dizon.)

Following World War II and until the 1960s, Filipinos lived in segregated neighborhoods, often finding it hard to buy homes from people who resisted selling to a "person of color." The Fulgencio family persevered and was one of the first Filipino families to live in the desirable College Park neighborhood. Visitacion Pabelico Fulgencio is shown here in front of her home in College Park on Redwing Street, c. 1969. (Courtesy of Rena Fulgencio.)

The wedding reception of Mr. and Mrs. Don Venoya was held at the San Pablo Lodge on Georgia Street in 1942. The couple had to get married in Washington State because it was illegal for Filipinos to marry Caucasians in California. (Courtesy of Filipino-American National Historical Society–Vallejo Chapter.)

This c. 1960 photo shows the exterior view of the Fellowship United Methodist Church's new sanctuary located at 218 Capitol Street. The sanctuary was completed in 1957 and moved to its current Beverly Hills, South Vallejo, location in the late 1960s when downtown Vallejo was redeveloped. (Courtesy of Fellowship United Methodist Church.)

The majority of Filipinos are of the Catholic faith, and the local churches ministered to the community by bringing in Filipino priests. In this March 1993 photo, Father Pol Gumapo of St. Vincent's Church gives Holy Communion at a Filipino Thanksgiving Mass. (Courtesy of *Vallejo Times-Herald*.)

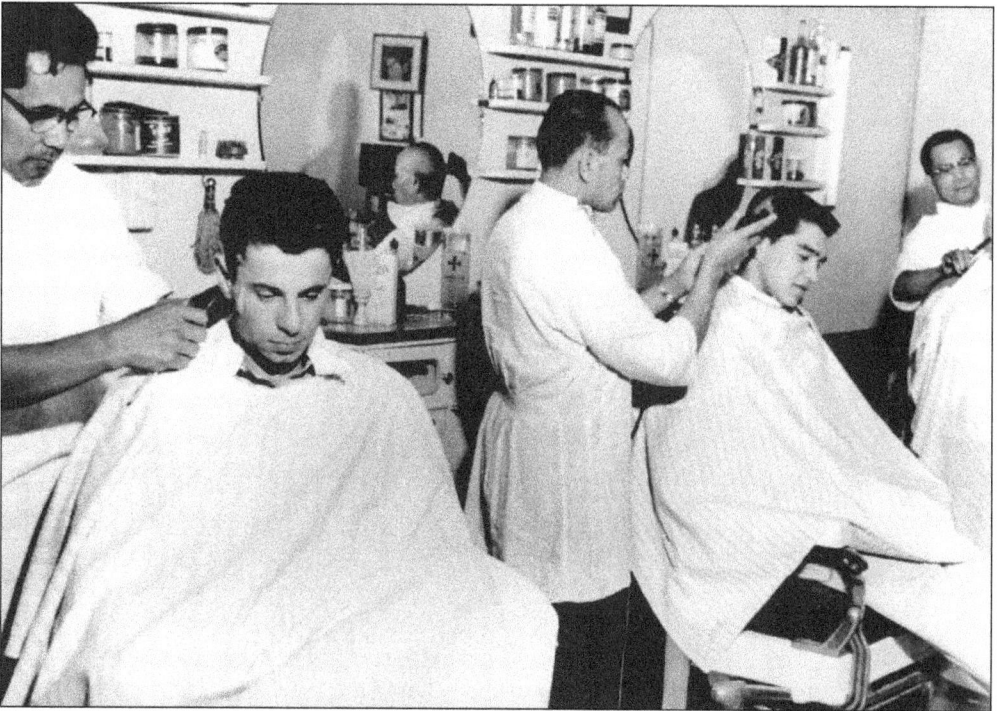

Lower Georgia Street was Vallejo's "Manilatown," where Filipino businesses flourished. Alex Difuntorum had a busy barbershop in that area. Filipinos were always well groomed and barbershops were important gathering places c. 1950. (Courtesy of the Filipino-American National Historical Society–Vallejo Chapter.)

Friends gather at a local supper club, c. 1941. Seated, from left to right, are Louis Lopez, Lucy Dizon (fourth), and Perfecto Bandalan (seventh). (Courtesy of Julie Dizon.)

As the number of Filipino families grew, their children became a generation of native-born Californians. Here members of the Legionarios del Trabajo hold a group baptism at the Veteran's Memorial Building, c.1950. (Courtesy of Nazario Orpilla.)

Philippine Consul General Romeo Arguelles attends the ribbon cutting ceremony for the Philippine House, located on Sonoma Boulevard. Pictured c. 1978, from left to right, are Joan Bennett, Consul General Arguelles, Ubaldo Flores (owner), Mrs. Arguelles, Mayor Florence Douglass, and Patrick O'Leary. (Courtesy of Vallejo Times-Herald.)

One of the most active groups in Vallejo was the Fellowship United Methodist Church Filipino Women's Club. The club held a number of fundraisers each year and raised money for the church's new building, c. 1953. (Courtesy of Fellowship United Methodist Church.)

Solano Community College started out as Vallejo Junior College. Many Filipinos attended the college after it moved to Suisun City. The Tayo Tayo Club, a Filipino student organization at Solano Community College, held many dances with live bands. Alma Hollinsead (bottom left) was a counselor and club advisor, c. 1977 (Courtesy of *Vallejo Times-Herald*.)

Pictured at the Grand Ball of the La Union Club of Vallejo, c. 1965, from left to right, are (front row) Dorie Nunez, ? Dulay, Charing Villanueva, Consuela Ancheta, and Betty Patacsil; (back row) Maurice Ancheta, ? Dulay, unidentified, unidentified, Nazario Orpilla, unidentified, Barney Villanueva, Maurice Fusilero, and unidentified. (Courtesy of Nazario Orpilla.)

Many Filipinos in Vallejo were fortunate to own their own homes. Most were able to afford them due to their employment at Mare Island Naval Shipyard or service in the military. The Rumbaoa family owned this home at 1032 Fifth Street. Pictured c. 1958, from left to right, are Eva Rumbaoa, Filomena Calilan, Florie Rumbaoa, and Venus Rumbaoa. (Courtesy of Florie Rumbaoa Barnett.)

The Filipino-American Chamber of Commerce is a very active business organization that holds mixers and breakfast meetings. Pictured c. 1994, from left to right, are (front row) Pilar Dumlao, Elori Mabolo, Sophie Pasibe, and Ellen Gabriel Lasa; (back row) Apin Celones, Mary Bitagon, Benny Manalang Jr., Tita Quintos, and Gloria Abad. (Courtesy of *Vallejo Times-Herald*.)

This Filipino-American Catholic Club installation of officers was held on February 18, 1974, at St. Vincent's cafeteria. Pictured, from left to right, are (front row) Feliciano Munar, Roque Paa, and Aploniario Dulay; (back row) Feliciano Munar, Juan Pascua, Eufemio Ducay, Catalino Bitagon, and Eufemio Ducay. (Courtesy of the Vallejo Naval and Historical Museum.)

Members of the Vallejo Filipino Women's Club attend their annual picnic at Blue Rock Springs Park, c. 1952. (Courtesy of Nazario Orpilla.)

Lucy Dizon became one of the richest women in Vallejo after World War II due to her business interests on Georgia Street and elsewhere. She was one of the few Filipinas who socialized outside of the Filipino community. In this c. 1958 photo, Dizon (at right) and an unidentified woman pose at Casa Blanca, located at 1524 Solano Avenue. (Courtesy of Julie Dizon.)

47

As the Filipino community grew, so did the number of organizations. Most were associated with Philippine regions or towns. In this photo, the La Union Club of Vallejo installs their officers at an event at the Eagle's Hall in 1965. Pictured, from left to right, are (front row) Apolinaro Dulay, Betty Patacsil, Teodora Nunez, Feliciano Munar, Consuelo Ancheta, Paulino Ogay, and Genaro Vergara; (back row) Joe Guererro, Sam Dulay, Nazario Orpilla, Pete Ventura, Maurice Ancheta, Maurice Fusilero, and Dionisio Kugo. (Courtesy of *Vallejo Times-Herald*.)

Queen contests are social functions as well as major fundraisers for the numerous Filipino organizations in Vallejo. The winner of the queen contest is the contestant who sells the most tickets with half the earnings going to the sponsoring organization and the other half to the contestant. Here, Norma Placido, contestant for Mrs. Filipino Community in August 1983, poses for the camera. (Courtesy of *Vallejo Times-Herald*.)

48

The Filipino Community of Solano County Inc. helped raise money in 1977 for its building fund. Pictured, from left to right, are guest of honor State Senator John Dunlap along with Mayor Florence Douglas, Catalina Paa, and James Coakley. Community activist Helen Marquez stands in front. (Courtesy of the Vallejo Naval and Historical Museum.)

This La Union Club party was held at the Eagle's Hall on Sonoma Boulevard, c. 1965. Today, the Eagle's Hall is home to the Iglesia Ni Cristo Filipino Church. (Courtesy of Nazario Orpilla.)

The Filipino-American Political Association meets with local political candidates in September 1968. Pictured, from left to right, are (front row) Dan Mazzoni, assemblyman John Dunlap, Bob Scofield, and R. Rath; (back row) Abe Tapia, Dr. Alfonso Aliga, Louis Flores, Richard Solarzano, and Stanley Garibay. (Courtesy of *Vallejo Times-Herald*.)

Evelyn Rillera, with her daughter Heather, and Mrs. Richard Bayquen, with little Lisa Randall, prepare for the Fellowship United Methodist Church's Bamboo Fair in 1958. (Courtesy of Fellowship United Methodist Church.)

Each year the Filipino-American Catholic Club hosted a dinner to raise funds for a leper colony headed by Father Hofstee. Here, cooks prepare for the annual Father Hofstee dinner in April 1978. Pictured, from left to right, are (front row) ? Nitalan, Amadeo Ramos, and Feliciano Munar; (back row) Roy Marinas and Catalino Bolaza. (Courtesy of the Vallejo Naval and Historical Museum.)

This Filipino community event featured the prettiest Filipinas in Vallejo. Included in the group are Dorothy Galiste, Maria Thamey, Norma Thamey, Corazon DeCarlo, Virgie Agasa, and Isabel Nifalar, pictured c. 1969. (Courtesy of the Galiste family.)

The Filipino-American Political Association accepts new members in this photo taken in September 1968. Pictured, from left to right, are Sinforoso Aparis, new member Dan Asera, Dr. Alfonso Aliga, new member Cosmedine Quilente, Ubaldo Flores, and Eufemio Ducay. (Courtesy of *Vallejo Times-Herald*.)

Vallejo Mayor Florence Douglas hosts a delegation from the Philippine Consul's office. Standing, from left to right, are Feliciano Munar, president of the Filipino Community, Philippine Consul General Romeo Arguelles, Mayor Ramon Bagatsing of Manila, Mayor Douglas, Solano County Supervisor Larry Asera, and Mrs. Bagatsing, *c.* 1977. (Courtesy of the Vallejo Naval and Historical Museum.)

Four

PATRIOTISM

Filipinos joined the war effort both as active duty Army or Navy personnel and civilian employees of Mare Island Naval Shipyard in Vallejo. Many sailors who came to Mare Island and explored Vallejo and its growing Filipino community eventually decided to make Vallejo their home. Here, George and Edward Dizon pose on Georgia Street, which catered to sailors on "shore leave," c. 1954. (Courtesy of Julie Dizon.)

The American Legion's Manuel L. Quezon Post 603 poses in front of the Veteran's Memorial Building in 1996. Commander Ben Contreras is seated in the front row in the middle, wearing sunglasses. (Courtesy of Jaime Juanillo.)

In addition to the Navy, some Filipinos served in one of the Army's all Filipino regiments. Faustino Bacus of Vallejo is pictured here in the middle of this 1940 photograph at Fort Ord. A member of the U.S. Army's Filipino Infantry Battalion, Bacus was at Fort Ord for Army training. (Courtesy of Pat Bacol Mendoza.)

Vallejo resident Aurelio Fulgencio, Senior Chief Officer E-8, is saluted after making rank on board the USS *Hancock* CVA-19, based in Oakland. (Courtesy of Rena Fulgencio.)

Mare Island Naval Shipyard was the magnet that brought Filipinos to Vallejo, either as servicemen or as civilian employees. A job at Mare Island guaranteed financial stability. Filipinos took pride in the fact that their efforts were helping in the defense of our country. Feliciano Aranda (far right) places cartridges in containers in Building A-73 in July 1955. (Courtesy of the Mare Island Historic Park Foundation–Peggy O'Drain.)

In 1946, the United States granted Filipinos the right to become American citizens. A citizenship class was started in Vallejo to serve all those wanting to study for the exams. Shown attending a class in 1947 are Clemente and Manuela Orpilla (second couple from the left) and Bernardo Bacol and Esparanza Bacol with their daughter Pat (far right). (Courtesy of Pat Bacol Mendoza.)

This American citizenship celebration was held in Vallejo in 1947. (Courtesy of Pat Bacol Mendoza.)

Victor Fernandez (kneeling in front) came to America in 1931. He enlisted in the U.S. Army in 1941 and, as a private first class, was assigned to the anti-tank company as a driver. (Courtesy of Nieves Fernandez.)

This c. 1960 group shot shows workers at Mare Island Naval Shipyard. Filipino employees worked as laborers, riggers, painters, and various other skilled and non-skilled positions. (Courtesy of Filipino-American National Historical Society–Vallejo Chapter.)

Like many of his countrymen, Nazario Orpilla joined the U.S. Navy when war was declared. Nazario was already working as a civilian employee at Mare Island Naval Shipyard when he joined in 1942. Serving as a steward, he was assigned to an admiral in Pearl Harbor, Hawaii. Four years later, in 1946, he was deemed too old at the age of 40 to re-enlist, so he returned to work at Mare Island. Racial occupational stereotypes relegated Filipinos in the Navy to steward status until the 1960s. (Courtesy of Nazario Orpilla.)

Navy Chief Steward Frank Linayen retires from the U.S. Navy at Mare Island Naval Shipyard after 25 years of dedicated service. Filipinos served primarily as stewards in the Navy after World War II and until the 1960s. (Courtesy of *Vallejo Times-Herald*.)

In 2003, the Filipino-American National Historical Society hosted the documentary film *Untold Triumphs* about the First and Second Filipino Infantry Battalions during World War II. Pete Serrano (seated in front) was a member of the battalion. Standing in back are the sons and daughter of former members of the battalion and include, from left to right, Ted Aranas, Pete Serrano Jr., and Jane Ajero. (Courtesy of Mel Orpilla.)

The screening of *Untold Triumphs* brought out one of the largest crowds ever to attend the Vallejo Naval and Historical Museum. Former battalion member Gregorio "George" Santos (in wheelchair) was in attendance, as were, in the back row, from left to right, Mel Orpilla and George Santos's daughters, Edlyn and Carmella. (Courtesy of Mel Orpillla.)

Santiago Quinto was born on July 20, 1909. This picture was taken in 1935, when 26-year-old Santiago was a private in the U.S. Army's First Infantry Battalion. (Courtesy of Nieves Fernandez.)

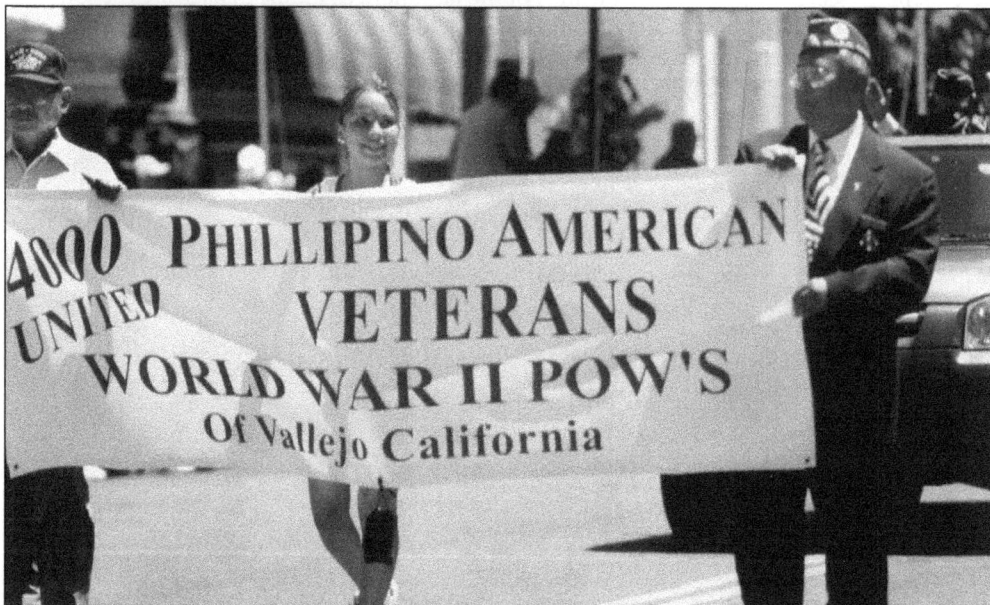

4000 UNITED PHILLIPINO AMERICAN VETERANS WORLD WAR II POW'S Of Vallejo California

The 1990 Immigration and Nationality Act allowed scores of Filipino World War II veterans entry into America to apply for citizenship—the United State's first step toward making amends for the 1946 Rescission Act, which denied benefits to Filipinos who served in the Philippine Commonwealth Army under the U.S. military. In response, many veterans made their way to Vallejo, where housing was inexpensive and family was close by. This group participated in the Fourth of July parade in 2004 and was led by Jaime Juanillo (far right) and Marino Aquisap (far left). (Courtesy of Mel Orpilla.)

This photo of the Navy crew of the USS *Enterprise* CVAN 65 was taken in 1983 and features the supply department with Charles Castillo at bottom front right and Julius Cresenis, also of Vallejo, in the third row on the right. Charles currently owns a barbershop on Sonoma Boulevard. (Courtesy of Charles Castillo.)

Lorenzo Calica retired from Mare Island Naval Shipyard in 1970 after working there for over 20 years. Many of the Filipino old-timers, the "Manongs," worked at Mare Island for more than 30 years before retiring. (Courtesy of Emily Calica.)

Fred Fernandez of Shop 72 carefully adjusts the spokes to straighten the rear wheel of a "patient" in August 1968. With 1,500 shipyard bicycles to maintain and repair, he usually had a full waiting room. Bicycles were the main form of transportation on the shipyard between shops. (Courtesy of the Mare Island Historic Park Foundation–Peggy O'Drain.)

Felimon Ladiero re-enlists in 1980 on board the USS Hector AR-7, whose homeport was at Mare Island Naval Shipyard. Commander Wysouri presents him with an honorable discharge certificate with his wife, Linda Ladiero, at his side. (Courtesy of Felimon Ladiero.)

This group photo of Mare Island Naval Shipyard's public works department was taken in 1948. (Courtesy of Vallejo Naval and Historical Museum.)

Louis Lopez and Richard Cantorna, members of the American Legion's Manuel L. Quezon Post 603, pose with their arms c. 1959. (Courtesy of *Vallejo Times-Herald*.)

In this 1949 photo, two unidentified Filipino sailors pose in front of the Mabuhay Restaurant located on Sonoma Boulevard near Lemon Street. The sign lists various Filipino delicacies being served that day, including *pancit*, *lumpia*, *dinuguan* (or "chocolate meat"), *sinigang*, and *pritada*. (Courtesy of Julie Dizon.)

Waving American and California flags, the citizenship class of 1947 poses for a group picture. Filipinos became more accepted as a group after the war because the Philippines was now a United States ally. (Courtesy of Filipino-American National Historical Society.)

Employees at Mare Island Naval Shipyard worked in various "shops" laid out on the island. Mare Island built the first atomic submarine and numerous other subs, boats, and ships. In this *c.* 1955 photo, Pio Velasco (ninth from left top row) works in the Mare Island Sail Loft, Building 55. (Courtesy of the Vallejo Naval and Historical Museum.)

The parents of Army Sgt. Victor Enderiz are presented with his Republic of Vietnam's Military Merit Medal, the Gallantry Cross, and the U.S. Bronze Star. The presentations were made by Col. John Donaldson Jr. to his father, Victor Enderiz Sr., and his mother, Erlinda Duenas. Sergeant Enderiz was a 1965 graduate of Vallejo High School and was killed in battle on December 2, 1967. (Courtesy of *Vallejo Times-Herald*.)

Joe Camacho and Jesse Wilson are hard at work on Mare Island in 1991. (Courtesy of the Vallejo Naval and Historical Museum.)

This Manuel L. Quezon Post 603 group photo was taken in 1960. (Courtesy of Nazario Orpilla.)

Alberto Pascual poses on the USS *Vega*, home ported in Alameda. Pascual was a storekeeper in 1965. Pascual moved his family to Vallejo in the early 1960s and is currently enjoying his retirement. (Courtesy of the Pascual family.)

The founding members of the Filipino-American Retired U.S. Armed Forces Association (FARUSAFA) pose in front of Grant School in South Vallejo on April 1959. Pictured, from left to right, are (front row) C. Bulatao, N. Gonzalez, F. Munar, A. Chavez, A. Aparis, B. Tamayo, E. Adoptante, R. Paa, and M. Aranas; (back row) A. Trinidad, C. Pascua, A. Bustamante, and I. Rumbaoa. Not pictured are Louis Lopez, P. Dandoy, and C. Bolasa. (Courtesy of Florie Rumbaoa Barnett.)

The staff of the Mare Island Medical Clinic are shown in 1996, when the naval base closed. (Courtesy of the Mare Island Historic Park Foundation–Peggy O'Drain.)

Five

GROWING UP IN VALLEJO

Before World War II, the number of Filipino families in Vallejo was small. After the war, many of the bachelor Filipinos went to the Philippines to be married, and brought their brides back to Vallejo, adding to the number of Filipino families. A Filipino Brownie troop was formed in 1942 because Filipino girls were not allowed to participate with the "white" Brownies. Among the members are Pat and Juanita Bacol, Ester and Lilly Reyes, and Lydia Guilling. (Courtesy of Pat Bacol Mendoza.)

Five graduating seniors received scholarships from the Filipino Community of Solano County in 1975. Pictured, from left to right, are (front row) Phillip Magalong, Judy Quichoy, and club president Feliciano Munar; (back row) Belinda Flores, Randy Bumatay, and Maria Chavez. (Courtesy of the Vallejo Naval and Historical Museum.)

There were only two Filipinos in Lincoln Elementary School's sixth-grade class in 1942: Fay Reyes (second row from top, sixth from left) and Juanita Bacol (third row from top, second from right). (Courtesy of Pat Bacol Mendoza.)

The Filipino Methodist Church was created to minister to Vallejo's Filipino children, who were not always welcome in other churches. The Youth Fellowship of the Filipino Methodist Church was organized by Mrs. Helen Marquez in early 1950. (Courtesy of the Fellowship United Methodist Church.)

Queen Scarlett Bazaar and her court wait their turn during Vallejo's Fourth of July parade, c. 1966. (Courtesy of the Galiste family.)

Eric Dumalag and Carissa Villanueva perform a swing dance at Vallejo's Unity Day Festival in 2001. Carissa is the daughter of Chris Villanueva, former Vallejo City Council member. (Courtesy of Mel Orpilla.)

Guests at Arlene Calica's birthday in 1957 at 817 Branciforte Street, from left to right, included (front row) Linda Cabatic, Leo Orpilla, Emila Ancheta, and Edwin Busto; (middle row) unidentified, Anita Ducay, Arlene Calica, Pricilla Evangelista, Belinda Florendo, Caroline Estigoy, and Linda Busto; (back row) Vincent Fusilero, Alice Patacsil, Lori Cabatic, Marlene Fusilero, and Imelda Evangelista. (Courtesy of Emily Calica.)

This group of third-generation Filipino kids formed a band called Just Us that performed all over Vallejo and Solano County. The band, from left to right, included (front row) Andre Calbert; (middle row) Danika Revelo, Joyette Acebedo, Serena Rillera, and Stevie Landaker; (back row) Lorena Fulgencio, Lynette Acebedo, Daniel Calbert, and Yvette Acebedo, c.1988 (Courtesy of Rena Fulgencio.)

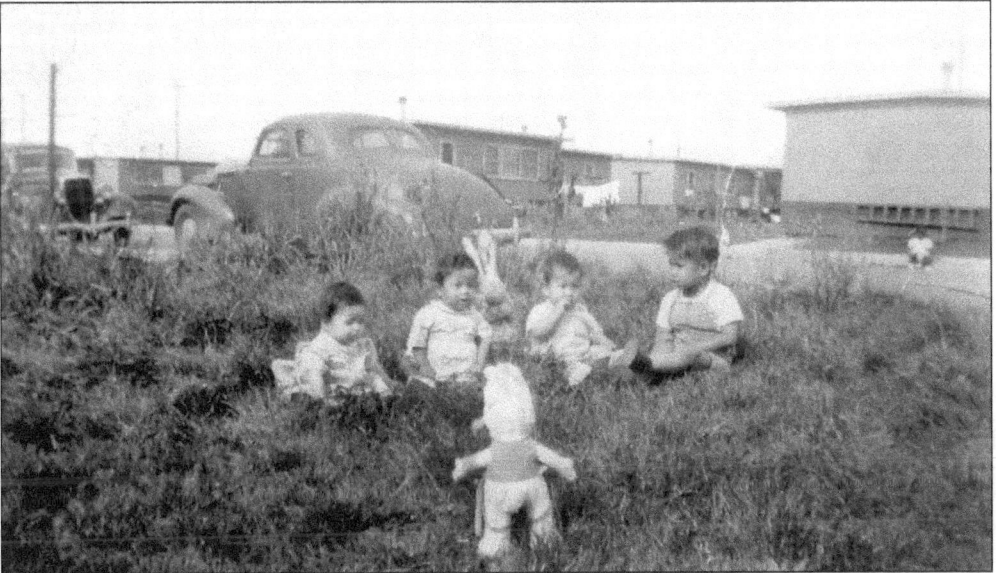

Filipino toddlers sit in the front yard of 207 Hood Street at Chabot Acres housing project. In this c. 1944 photo are Ray Lontayo (second from left), Gilbert Caballero, and Mel Caballero. (Courtesy of Daniel Tiburcio.)

In this c. 1975 photo, Lonette Quenga plays beanbag toss at Cave Elementary School's summer recreation program while Kim Apilado (far right) watches. (Courtesy of *Vallejo Times-Herald*.)

The Veterans Memorial Building ballroom was the setting for many Filipino dances and parties until its closing in the 1980s due to asbestos issues. Here Betty Galope and Shirley Galope pose at the top of the steps, c. 1949. (Courtesy of the Galiste family.)

Florie Rumbaoa poses for the camera, c. 1960. A noted Polynesian dance instructor, Florie and her family immigrated to America in the late 1950s. (Courtesy of Florie Rumbaoa Barnett.)

Emily Calica poses at her house on 106 Starr Avenue in 1968. She was a student at St. Vincent's High School and recalls getting demerits for wearing her skirts too short. (Courtesy of Emily Calica.)

Lincoln Elementary School's fourth-grade class in 1942 had only three Filipinos: Charles Bansuelo (second row, fourth from left), Pat Bacol (top row, third from right), and Esther Reyes (second row from top, third from right). (Courtesy of Pat Bacol Mendoza.)

Members of the Pilipino Youth Coalition pose at the newly opened Unity Plaza at the foot of Georgia Street in 2004. Inlaid in the cement is a Filipino proverb that says, "To know where you are going, you must first look at where you came from." (Courtesy of Mel Orpilla.)

Pilipino Youth Coalition members ham it up at their annual picnic at Blue Rock Springs Park in August 2004. Pictured, from left to right, are Napier Bulanan, Darah Macaraeg, Michael Yra, and Alaric Sales. (Courtesy of Mel Orpilla.)

Single Filipina women being courted by sailors visiting Mare Island Naval Shipyard pose at Blue Rock Springs Park in 1962. The women, from left to right, are Julie Dizon, Florie Rumbaoa, Lolita Palle, Norma Aparis, Cora Apilado, Eva Rumbaoa, unidentified, and Adele Madayag. (Courtesy of Julie Dizon.)

Felipe LaCosta, Ray Lontayo, and Samuel LaCosta are shown here at Chabot Acres housing project, *c.* 1945. (Courtesy of Daniel Tiburcio.)

Kathy Barreto and Glen Dayrit play in the rolling barrel during Filipino Day at Children's Wonderland Park in 1983. (Courtesy of *Vallejo Times-Herald*.)

Marcella and Rosie Fabillaran pose for the camera at Blue Rock Springs Park, c. 1964. (Courtesy of Marcella Thurmon.)

Sheena Minoc emcees a Pilipino Youth Coalition fundraiser and talent showcase entitled "Flip'd Roots" in 2002 at the Fetterly Playhouse Theater as the rest of the members look on. (Courtesy of Belle Orpilla.)

Alice Carter was one of the first native Filipino Vallejoans. She was born in 1915 at 233 Florida Street to her Filipina mother, Maria, and her African-American father, George Washington Carter. Carter fought in the Philippine-American War. (Courtesy of Alice Realiza.)

Filipino teens posing in front of the War Memorial c. 1959, from left to right, are (front row) Patricia Orpilla, unidentified, Cristen Orpilla, unidentified, and Virginia Orpilla; (back row) Jimmy Hullana, Mary Hullana, unidentified, and Nazario Orpilla. (Courtesy of FANHS Vallejo Chapter.)

In this 1943 photo, Daniel Tiburcio plays with his dog and "horse" at the Chabot Acres housing project. (Courtesy of Daniel Tiburcio.)

This c. 1959 photo was taken on the 100 block of Carolina Street with Tony Madayag in the car's passenger seat. Sitting on top of the car, from left to right, are Julie Dizon and Bessie Aganon. Standing watch is Cora Apilado. (Courtesy of Julie Dizon.)

Elsa Widenmann Elementary School students Taryn Lizama, 12 years old (left), and Kathy Fernandez, 10 years old (right), practice for the All-City Band Day in 1991. Filipino youth gravitate toward many of the musical programs offered in the school district, including band, drum corps, and drill teams. (Courtesy of *Vallejo Times-Herald*.)

These Filipino-American beauties, from left to right, are Francine Cordero, Leticia Mariano, and Erlinda Bigornia, c. 1955. (Courtesy of the Vallejo Naval and Historical Museum.)

This family celebration was held for Juhn Verano's graduation from San Francisco State University in 2001 after obtaining a master's degree in social work. The four generations featured here, from left to right, include (first row) Desi Galiste, Symone Wright, and Angelique Galiste; (second row) Lionel Galiste, Flo Verano, and Florlinda Verano; (third row) Alex Verano, Dorothy Galiste Ross, Tonia Galiste, and Juhn Verano; (fourth row) Joe Gumataotao, Chris Chism, Mike Fedyna, Merna Galiste Fedyna, Corey Chism, Joe Galiste, David Galiste, and Edie Galiste.

Melissa Arzaga, a member of the Filipino Task Force's Youth Internship Project, shares the results of the project's community-wide youth survey in 1992. The survey provided information on issues affecting Filipino youth, such as teen pregnancy, drug use, gangs, and parental relationships. (Courtesy of Mel Orpilla.)

Second-generation Filipino-American youth formed basketball teams for recreation in towns up and down California. In this photo, the Vallejo Val Phi basketball team receives a trophy from Don Gleason of the *Vallejo Times-Herald*. Pictured here *c.* 1955, from left to right, are (front row) Bud Ganalon, Frank Delgado, John Reyes, Hank Dacuyan, unidentified, and unidentified; (back row) George Oriate, Ted Sarmiento, Don Delacerna, Eddie Chavez, Norma Difuntorum, Krispin Selim, Don Gleason, unidentified, unidentified, and Paul Espejo. (Courtesy of FANHS Vallejo Chapter.)

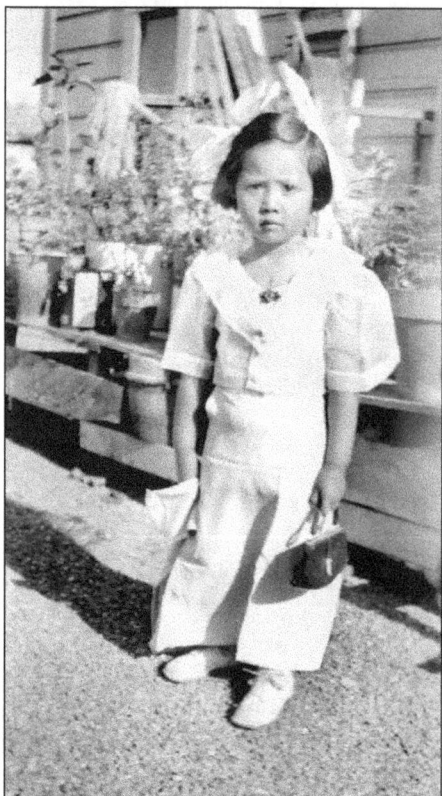

Four-year-old Pat Bacol, in her finest Filipiniana dress, is ready to walk in Vallejo's 1939 Fourth of July parade. (Courtesy of Pat Bacol Mendoza.)

The Mabuhay Filipino Adults Club's (MAFILA) Hawaiian dance troupe prepares to perform for the Second Annual International Dance Festival in August 1972. Pictured, from left to right, are (front row) Marian Hopwood and Debbie De La Cerna; (back row) Maria Thamy, Loretta De La Cerna, and Dorothy Galiste. (Courtesy of *Vallejo Times-Herald*.)

This children's Bible study class in 1953 was held at the future site of the Filipino Methodist Church located at 218 Capitol Street. (Courtesy of Fellowship United Methodist Church.)

The Filipino Methodist Church youth hobby group learns how to make baskets in 1951, when the church was originally located on Capitol Street. (Courtesy of Fellowship United Methodist Church.)

Francine Cordero, seated third from left, grew up in South Vallejo, which was a multi-cultural neighborhood. This photo was taken c. 1955. (Courtesy of Zacarias Cordero.)

The Filipino-American Progressive Organization's 1977 debutantes, from left to right, were (front row) Emma Nunez, Susan Cortez, Vicky Generao, Eileen Alfonso, and Joyce Pagala; (back row) Pinky Rostrata, Dorleen Lastra, Alice Reyes, and Yvonne Berenguer. (Courtesy of *Vallejo Times-Herald*.)

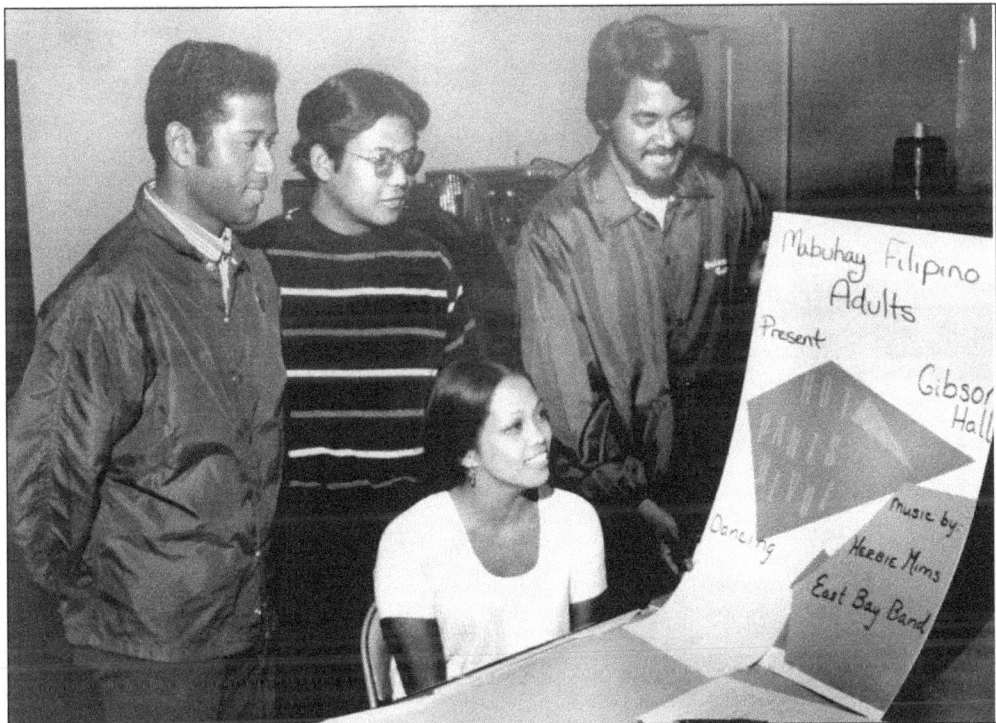

The Mabuhay Filipino Adults Club (MAFILA) readies for their one-day conference at Gibson Hall at the Solano County Fairgrounds in 1971. Seated in front is Marian Hopwood. Standing, from left to right, are Roger Bolaza, Fred Munar, and Cesar Alemania. (Courtesy of *Vallejo Times-Herald*.)

In this c. 1989 photo, Michelle Pineda prepares for her cotillion, a traditional coming-of-age party where a young woman who turns 18 is formally introduced to society. (Courtesy of *Vallejo Times-Herald*.)

James Cruz, Ho Sung, and Neil Cabreza pass the time waiting for the female half of the cotillion to finish getting ready, as Sonny Talag adjusts his tie, c. 1989. (Courtesy of *Vallejo Times-Herald*.)

Lenci Landaker won the 100-pound weight class California State Wrestling Championship two years in a row (2001 and 2002) and placed fourth in the 2002 nationals. Before her, Mark Munoz, also a Filipino and graduate of Vallejo High School, was the first wrestler from Vallejo to win a state championship. Mark continued to excel in collegiate wrestling, winning a national championship and trying out for the Olympics. (Courtesy of Rena Fulgencio.)

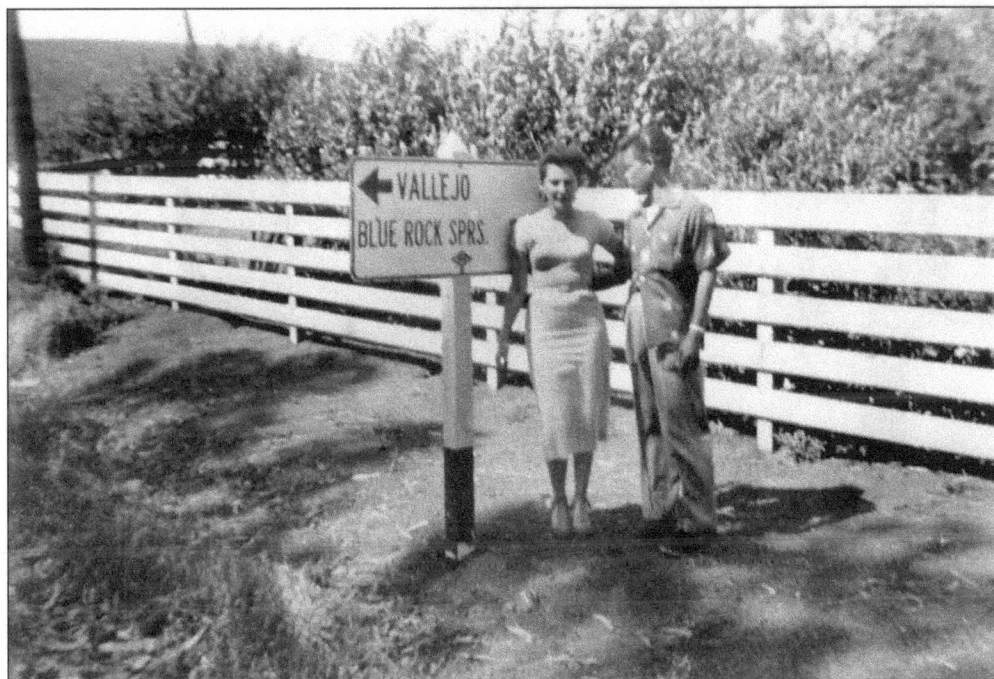

A couple poses on Columbus Parkway in East Vallejo at the sign pointing to Blue Rock Springs Park, c. 1955. (Courtesy of Filipino-American National Historical Society–Vallejo Chapter.)

Revelers at the 1960 New Year's Eve celebration at the Galiza house on Pennsylvania Street, from left to right, included (front row) Venus Rumbao; (middle row) Florie Rumbaoa, Filomena Calilan, Lita Galutira, and Delfin ?; (back row) Eva Rumbaoa and Fred Galiza. (Courtesy of Florie Rumbaoa Barnett.)

Members of the Makabayan Youth of Vallejo install their new officers during a public dance at the Dan Foley Cultural Center in June 1993. Pictured, from left to right, are Mary Ann Flores, Carlos Pajarillo, Rizal Robancho, and Riza Garabato. (Courtesy of *Vallejo Times-Herald*.)

Six

SHARING OUR CULTURE

Filipinos love to party and have a good time, and music, food, and entertainment usually go hand in hand. Filipinos brought cultural festivals and traditions from the islands to Vallejo, such as queen contests, which are still celebrated in Vallejo and in small towns throughout the Philippines and are a way to raise funds for various community or municipal projects. Winners are chosen not for their beauty or talent, but for raising the most money through ticket sales. Children are taught Filipino dances to carry on the tradition and share their culture in their new home. These Filipino dancers at the Solano County Fairgrounds on March 12, 1966, from left to right, include Nancy Maraña, Corazon DeCardo, Dorothy Galiste, Emily Ancheta, Mary Ann Parahinog, and Sotera Flores. (Courtesy of the Galiste family.)

Frank Verano and His Orchestra, from left to right, featured Frank Verano on guitar, Simeon LaCosta, Victor Enderiz, and Mr. Bascones. Seated are Lena Tanzo and Tonia Galiste, Verano's singers, c. 1953. (Courtesy of the Galiste family.)

Mrs. Edward Fahy crowns Queen Linda Pastor at the annual Coronation Ball sponsored by the Filipino-American Catholic Club on July 7, 1962. Her escort is Joseph Macapinlac and the attendants are Cathy Roldan and Mary Jane Torrijos. (Courtesy of the Filipino-American Catholic Club.)

Tonia Galiste sings at a Filipino community event in 1953. Juan Sarmiento is in the background. (Courtesy of the Galiste family.)

The band Sleque, featuring a group of Filipino kids, perform at the Vallejo Parent Nursery. On drums is Stevie Landaker, singing is Yvette Acebedo, and on keyboards is Loren Fulgencio with Lynette Acebedo in May 1987. (Courtesy of Rena Fulgencio.)

The Filipino-American Social Services organization participates in the 2000 Fourth of July parade, displaying the "Gigantes of Philippine History," which included Jose Rizal, Gabriela Silang, and Sari Manok. (Courtesy of Mel Orpilla.)

A "Jeepney" is displayed at the annual Philippine Independence Day Celebration at the Marina Vista Park in 1993. In the Philippines, Jeepneys are common modes of public transportation and were popularized after World War II when Filipinos found a creative way to recycle abandoned American Jeeps. (Courtesy of *Vallejo Times-Herald*.)

Philippine Day at the Solano County Fair features Queen Adele Bautista surrounded by members of the Filipino community, c. 1955. Queen contest winners were held in high esteem and were paraded for the public to see how beautiful Filipino women were. The queen contests were also major fundraisers for the sponsoring Filipino organization. Winners were chosen based on the amount of tickets sold and money raised by each contestant. The winner got to keep half of the money. The other half went to the sponsoring organization. (Courtesy of Filipino-American National Historical Society–Vallejo Chapter.)

The Filipino-American National Historical Society is a national organization with chapters in various states throughout the nation. "The mission of FANHS shall be to promote understanding, education, enlightenment, appreciation, and enrichment through the identification, gathering, preservation, and dissemination of the history and culture of Filipino Americans in the United States." Pictured in 1992, the charter members of the Filipino-American National Historical Society–Vallejo Chapter, from left to right, are (front row) Belle Santos, Linda Alemania, Lala Llacuna, and Helen Marquez; (back row) Mel Orpilla, Cesar Alemania, Juhn Verano, Cris Orpilla, Joe Fortes, Herb Rillera, Evelyn Rillera, and Fred Cordova, the godfather of Filipino-American history from Seattle. (Courtesy of Filipino-American National Historical Society–Vallejo Chapter.)

In this 1964 photo, Florie Rumbaoa, Ike Lozada, and Cindy ? pose on a Fourth of July float. Ike Lozada was a famous singer from the Philippines. (Courtesy of Florie Rumbaoa Barnett.)

Pictured c. 1955, this Vallejo-based band included Jack Jacildo (left, on bass guitar), Mauricio Calica (third from left), and Lorenzo Calica (fourth from left). (Courtesy of Emily Calica.)

The Persuasion Band was popular in the early 1970s, playing funk and soul at many parties and dances. Band members, from left to right, included Joe Cruz, Ron Carson, Tony Lopez, Eddie Lastra, and Faustino Gamulo. (Courtesy of *Vallejo Times-Herald*.)

St. Basil's Church has a large Filipino congregation and two Filipino deacons, including, from left to right, Robert Sims, an unidentified St. Basil's priest, and Leo Mangoba. This photo was taken c. 1996. (Courtesy of *Vallejo Times-Herald*.)

Robert Sims (far right) teaches a judo class for the Greater Vallejo Recreation District at the Dan Foley Cultural Center, c. 1990. (Courtesy of *Vallejo Times-Herald*.)

This crowning of Miss Philippines Solano County took place around 1965. (Courtesy of Filipino Community of Solano County.)

Sheila Fortuno is crowned Miss Filipino-American Catholic Club in 1977. Pictured, from left to right, are Joe Galiste, Laura Rodriguez, Sheila Fortuno, Cesar Fortuno, Evelyn Castanares, and Joey Bulozan. (Courtesy of *Vallejo Times-Herald*.)

This Filipino Community float was entered in the 1942 Fourth of July parade. At far right standing on the float, Little Juanita Bacol wears a Red Cross cap and holds onto the flagpole. (Courtesy of Pat Bacol Mendoza.)

Venus Rumbaoa was crowned Miss Visayas by the Filipino-American Catholic Club in 1968 and was featured in the Vallejo Fourth of July parade. Pictured, from left to right, are Jeannie Luzano, Laura Mertz, Venus Rumbaoa, and Marlene Fusilero. (Courtesy of Florie Rumbaoa Barnett.)

Sonny Hatsme trains kids at the Carquinez Heights housing project, c. 1950. Starting in 1941, he trained hundreds of young boxers in Vallejo and later coached boxers at the Police Activities League. He had an illustrious career as a boxer and, later in life, as a champion horseshoe pitcher. (Courtesy of the Vallejo Naval and Historical Museum.)

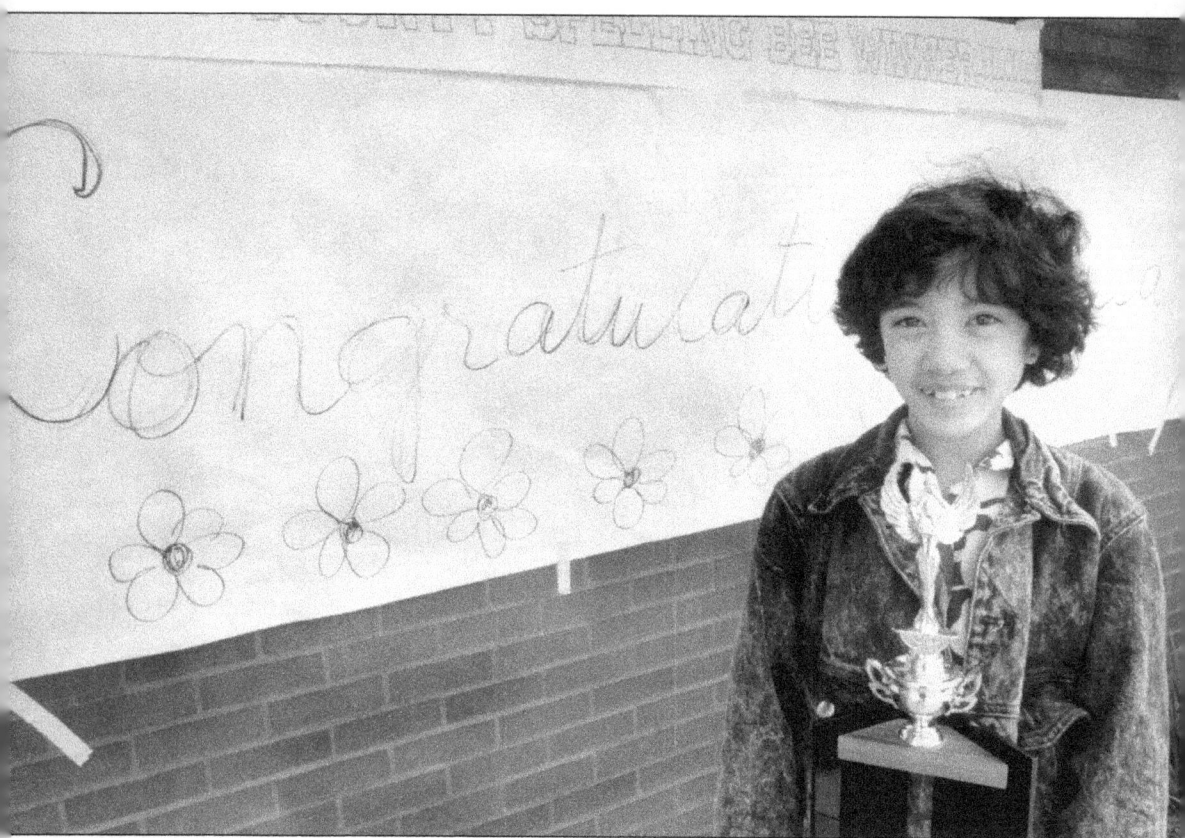

Melissa Abueg, an 11-year-old at Glen Cove Elementary School, wins the title of Solano County Spelling Bee Champ in 1989. (Courtesy of *Vallejo Times-Herald*.)

Roy and Aida Manasalan dance the Tinikling during Filipino Day at Children's Wonderland Park in 1983. This favorite cultural dance imitates the movement of the tikling birds as they walk between grass stems or run over tree branches. Dancers imitate the tikling bird's legendary grace and speed by skillfully maneuvering between large bamboo poles. (Courtesy of *Vallejo Times-Herald*.)

Ben Mariano, a pioneer Filipino in Vallejo, and his wife take a laugh break during the planning of Vallejo's Annual Philippine Independence Day in 1990. Filipinos in Vallejo chose the month of June for their annual celebration because the Philippines declared independence from Spain on June 12, 1898, after over 300 years of Spanish rule. The celebration continues on an even larger scale today, drawing over 10,000 guests over a two-day festival on the Vallejo waterfront. (Courtesy of *Vallejo Times-Herald*.)

Kajukenbo Self Defense Institute has been performing at the Solano County Fair for over 32 consecutive years. Posing at the county building on the fairgrounds are Frank Umipig, Carmie Umipig, Kathy Hodges, Butch Ercole, Kristina Ercole, and Sifu Emil Bautista, *c. 1976.* (Courtesy of Emil Bautista.)

Vallejo sprouted a number of karate and martial arts classes. Some were taught through the Greater Vallejo Recreation District. Here, karate instructor Bill Vargas (far right) teaches students Joan Vargas, Karen Lotridge, and Edie Monaghan the correct stances, *c. 1974.* (Courtesy of *Vallejo Times-Herald.*)

Filipinos always chose a high-ranking politician or his wife to crown the next queen. Being crowned a queen was a high distinction that carried considerable weight beyond the year of the winner's reign. Here Mrs. Robert Legget, wife of Assemblyman Robert Legget, presents Miss Philippines Marie Jane Luzano with a trophy in July 1961.

Norma Placido eventually won this contest. She continued serving the Filipino Community of Solano County by being elected its president in the late 1990s. Here she prepares for the Mrs. Filipino Community Queen Contest in August 1983. Pictured, from left to right, are Norma Placido, Marie Saqueton, Claro Mamaril, and Filipino Community President Feliciano Munar. (Courtesy of *Vallejo Times-Herald*.)

After decades of having non-Filipino politicians crown the queens, Vallejo finally got its first Filipino politician in Larry Asera. This is the coronation of Queen Nancy Luzano at a pageant at St. Vincent's Memorial Center in 1975. Assisting, from left to right, are Teresa Corpus, Glen Agasa, Fernando Amado, and City Councilman Larry Asera. (Courtesy of the Vallejo Naval and Historical Museum.)

With more young ladies going off to college, there was a shortage of contestants for the, so the name was changed to the Mrs. Philippines. Today there is never a shortage of women vying for the title. This photo shows the coronation of Queen Leilani Lennie Contreras Organo, Mrs. Philippines of Solano County, in 1992. Her attendants, from left to right, are Irene Ananciacion, Gertrude Bautista, her husband Simeon Organo, Bill Ananciacion, Jose Bautista, and Ben Contreras. (Courtesy of *Vallejo Times-Herald*.)

106

Seven

MODEL FILIPINO-
AMERICAN COMMUNITY

Rafael's Bar and Restaurant, located at 301 Nebraska Street, is the nucleus of the upscale hip-hop culture in Vallejo. The décor was designed by Rafael Santos Jr., a graduate of the San Francisco Academy of Arts. His brother, Joe Santos, manages the operation with the assistance of brother John in the kitchen. Every Thursday night the bar hosts "Listen and Be Heard," a spoken word, poetry, and music event, drawing the most diverse crowd in the city. The bar is owned by Rafael Sr. and Ester Santos, who also own and operate Rafael's Expert Catering. (Courtesy of Rafael Santos Jr.)

Filipino cowboys work at Lucy Dizon's Midway Ranch at the corner of Benica Road and Columbus Parkway. From left to right are Perfecto Bandalan, unidentified, unidentified, Larry Dizon, and Lino Dizon, c. 1946. Notice their classy riding outfits. Lucy owned the ranch with her husband. (Courtesy of Julie Dizon.)

Pastor Rey Bernardes (center) started the Christian Help Center over 20 years ago to aid the homeless in Vallejo. His ministry has since expanded to Mare Island where his church operates the Success Center. He has helped countless people and their families get back on their feet. (Courtesy of Pastor Rey Bernardes.)

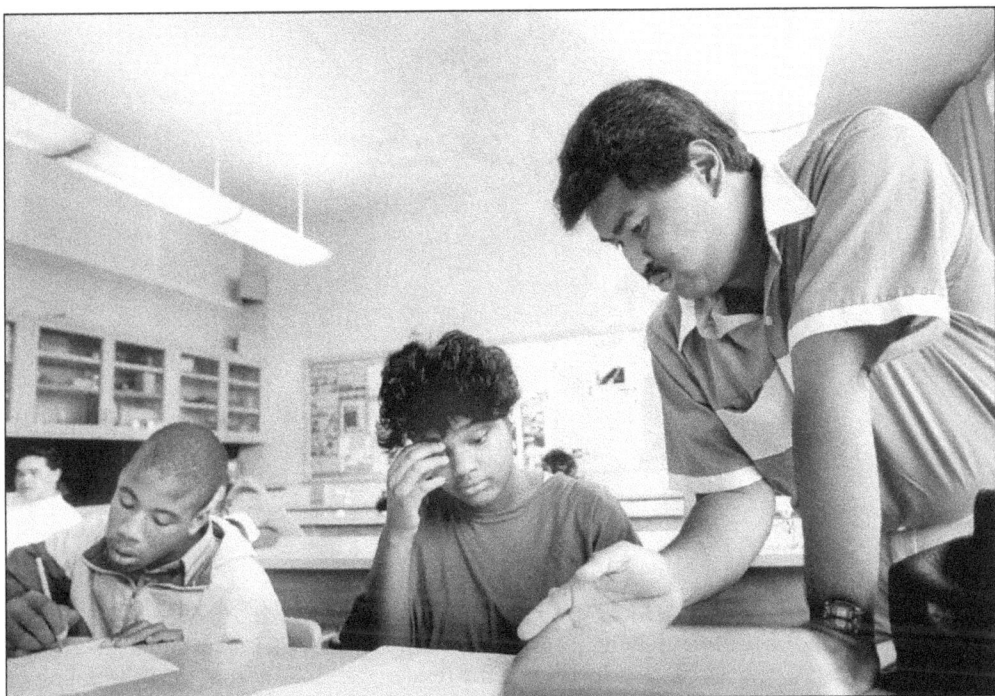

Mike Santos taught biology at Hogan High School in 1987, then went on to become the principal of Solano Middle School and then principal of Hogan in 2004. He was also the football coach at Hogan High School. Mike is respected throughout the school district for his dedication to his students and his staff. (Courtesy of *Vallejo Times-Herald*.)

Lisa Hullana, a second-generation Filipina, went from Hogan High School homecoming queen in 1974 to Hollywood. She was a professional model before appearing in several films and in the television show *Magnum P.I.* She is the granddaughter of Mary and Bernard Hullana, a pioneer Filipino family. Her mother, Evelyn, was a very successful real estate agent in Vallejo. Lisa now makes her home in Southern California. (Courtesy of *Vallejo Times-Herald*.)

Larry Asera, a third-generation Filipino, was the first Filipino in Vallejo's history to be elected to the Vallejo City Council. He won in 1973 at the tender age of 24, at that time the youngest city councilman in the State of California. His grandfather, Lorenzo Asera, was only 16 years old when he arrived in Hawaii to work on the sugarcane plantations. Larry is an example of the immigrant dream becoming a reality. (Courtesy of Larry Asera.)

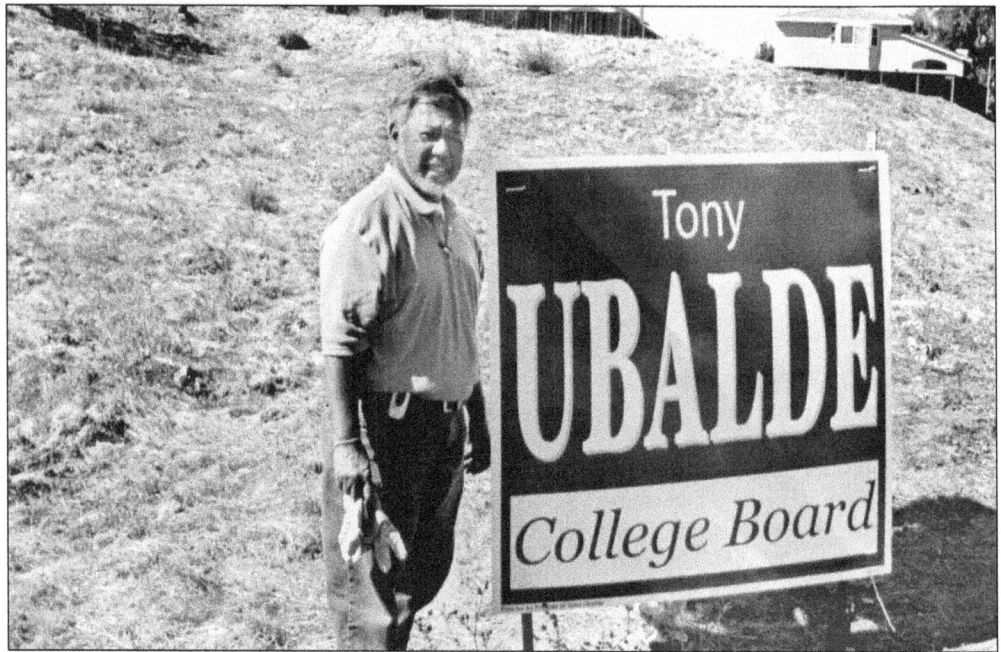

Tony Ubalde, retired pastor of Fellowship United Methodist Church, stands next to his campaign sign in 2004 during his race to win a seat on the Solano Community College Board of Trustees. He won the election and is the first Filipino on the board. (Courtesy of Mel Orpilla.)

110

Kaiser Permanente Hospital has a large Filipino staff, including doctors, nurses, and technicians. This group of employees, from left to right, are (front row) Nora Flores, Sue Alagon, Eileen Ajero, and Marion Cruz; (back row) Ernesto Zambrano, Agnes Solla, and Ed Dumaguin. (Courtesy of Ed Dumaguin.)

Filipinos have been part of the economic engine of Vallejo since the turn of the last century. The earliest Filipino businesses were on lower Georgia Street, although currently the Filipino business centers are at Vallejo Plaza (formerly Larwin Plaza) and the Springs Road corridor. In this c. 1950 photo, Lucy Dizon and Buddy Hugaldo pose in front of the Filipino-owned Pinales Serviceman's Café on lower Georgia Street. Lucy also had business interests on Georgia Street. (Courtesy of Julie Dizon.)

In this 2002 photo, Vallejo Pilipino Youth Coalition (PYC) member Rachel Solla participates in an anti-Iraq War rally in San Francisco. The PYC, a program of Filipino-American Social Services, teaches Filipino youth about their heritage, community involvement, and community organizing skills. (Courtesy of Mel Orpilla.)

Sonny Hatsme, a former boxing champ and boxing coach in his younger years, continued his competitive career by competing in horseshoe throwing. In 1977 he won the Northern California Horseshoe Championship. Sonny was featured on Channel 5's *Evening Magazine with Jan Yanehiro* program as a local hero. (Courtesy of *Vallejo Times-Herald*.)

Seafood City, a Filipino-owned grocery store chain based in San Diego, opened its first Northern California store in Vallejo in 2003. Its arrival, along with several popular Philippine-based restaurants such as Chow King and Max's of Manila, revitalized the former Larwin Plaza Shopping Center. It is now a destination for Filipinos from throughout the Bay Area. The once-dying shopping center is often so busy that finding a parking space is a problem. (Courtesy of Mel Orpilla.)

Mayor Tony Intintoli and City Councilman Larry Asera stand in front of the fountain in the plaza between the main post office and the JFK Library. The fountain was torn out in 2003 to make way for the Georgia Street extension to the waterfront. In its place is the Unity Plaza, dedicated to all the cultures in Vallejo. Larry Asera and Tony Intintoli continue their friendship today. (Courtesy of *Vallejo Times-Herald*.)

In 2000, Filipino political empowerment in Vallejo continued with the appointment of Belle Orpilla as the field representative for State Senator Wesley Chesbro. Belle had previously been the administrative assistant to the superintendent of Vallejo schools. She represents the senator at various governmental and community functions and events. (Courtesy of Mel Orpilla.)

Frank Acojido, the first Filipino principal in the Vallejo School District (Hogan High School), poses with Jacob Orpilla (left)and Athena Shingu (right) during the Hogan High School graduation in 1999. Since then, the school board has appointed a number of Filipino principals and administrators, including Mike Santos, Mabella Gonzalez, Myna Audal, and Marietta Tretasco. The Vallejo schools also teach Tagalog language courses in all of its high schools. (Courtesy of Mel Orpilla.)

The Luisa G. Evangelista Filipino Store on Sacramento Street was the only Filipino market during the late 1960s and 1970s after the redevelopment of lower Georgia Street closed down the last remaining Filipino businesses. Luisa Evangelista had an exclusive contract with the government to import goods from the Philippines for the military commissaries. Here she is shown arranging a display at her store in 1976. (Courtesy of Vallejo Naval and Historical Museum.)

Filipino senior citizens in Vallejo are not content to just sit around the house. Many events are planned to keep them busy. For instance, the Filipino America Senior Citizens of Solano County holds a Valentine's Day event at the Filipino Community Center each year. In 1982, the King and Queen of Hearts event selected Flora Incleto and Agripino Casanova as their recipients. In addition to this Filipino senior club, there is also the United Senior Citizens Association. (Courtesy of Jose Bautista.)

Nestor Aliga pushes his son, Rizal, during the Mare Island to Medusa 10K Race in 2002. The race helps raise money for local youth organizations. It starts on the Mare Island Bridge and ends at Six Flags Marine World. Nestor is a colonel in the Army Reserves and comes from the pioneer Aliga family. His grandfather, Eligio Aliga, came to America in 1926. His wife, Rozzana, was the first Filipino elected to the Vallejo School Board. (Courtesy of Mel Orpilla.)

Banana Q Restaurant at 301 Georgia Street is a popular eating-place for Filipinos living and working in downtown Vallejo. The restaurant's good food and low-cost meals provide many Filipino seniors with a good, hot meal each day. On the weekends it becomes a popular karaoke bar and dance club. It is most famous for its hot and sweet Senorita Rolls. Early in the morning the line heads out of the door as people come in for this local delicacy. Owners Nellie and Romy Maranan pose outside their establishment. (Courtesy of Mel Orpilla.)

Reginald Garcia was hired as Vallejo's first Filipino police officer in 1974. Reggie graduated from Vallejo High School and eventually became a lieutenant in the police force. Here he teaches gun safety to students at Steffan Manor Elementary School in January 1995. The Vallejo Police Department now employs a number of Filipino officers to better serve the community. They include Bob Sampayan, Rick Florendo, Lloyd Douglass, and Allan Caragan. (Courtesy of *Vallejo Times-Herald*.)

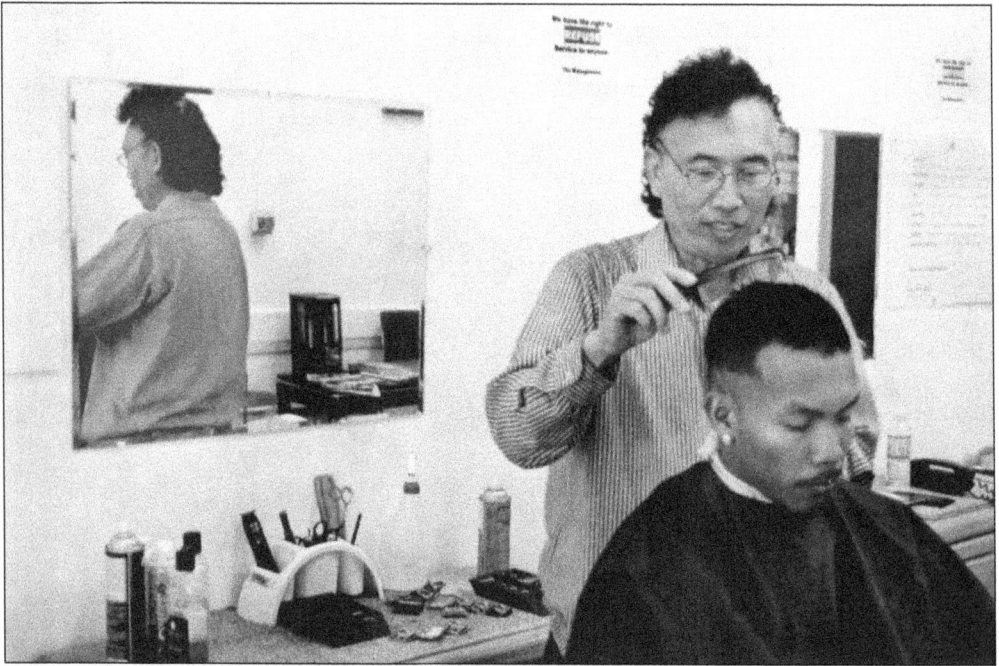

Historically, Filipino barbershops were where the men went to get their haircut but also where they caught up on local issues and gossip. Today Charles Cuts keeps that tradition alive in downtown Vallejo and owner Charles Castillo usually has a waiting list of appointments. Charles, who is retired from the U.S. Navy, is one of the last barbers to still use a straightedge razor to give the cleanest haircut. His shop is at 1725 Sonoma Boulevard. (Courtesy of Mel Orpilla.)

Pete Rey was elected vice mayor by the city council in 1999. He first ran for city council in 1991 and lost, then tried again in 1995 and lost again. Finally in 1997 he won, coming in second in a field of 12. He will be completing his second and final term as councilman in December 2005. Pete is a symbol of perseverance, providing leadership at a time when the Filipino community and Vallejo in general were experiencing tremendous growth. (Courtesy of Pete Rey, photo by Red Wetzel.)

The members of the Filipino Youth Internship Project of the Filipino Task Force conducted the first-ever Filipino youth survey in 1992. The Filipino Task Force was a program of Fighting Back Partnership and was funded by a federal grant that challenged Vallejo to be more inclusive of its ethnic communities in planning substance abuse prevention programs. Pictured, from left to right, are Charles Abad, Romina Vicente, Jeff Ragonton, Melissa Arzaga, Romer Blanquera, and Albert Asprer. (Courtesy of *Vallejo Times-Herald*.)

Filipino-American Social Services (FASS), the only Asian Pacific Islander social service agency in Solano County, encourages the youth of Vallejo to participate in community-wide events that Filipinos do not usually attend, such as the annual Dr. Martin Luther King Jr. parade. The youths learn that Dr. King fought and died for the rights of all people, including Filipinos. FASS has marched in the parade every year since its inception. Here Christopher Dacumos and E.J. Franco hold the FASS sign during the Martin Luther King Jr. Day Parade in 2001. (Courtesy of Mel Orpilla.)

Professional comedian Allan Manalo, a 1981 graduate of Vallejo High School, makes a joke at a benefit comedy show held at the Fetterly Theater in 2003. Allan is a pioneer Filipino stand-up comedian and mentors others who follow in his footsteps. He pokes fun at the Filipino culture, his family, and people who make fun of Filipinos. He has traveled all over the United States and the Philippines with his comedy act. He was also the creative genius behind the Filipino comedy troupe "Tongue in a Mood" and the manager of Bindlestiff Theater in San Francisco. (Courtesy of Mel Orpilla.)

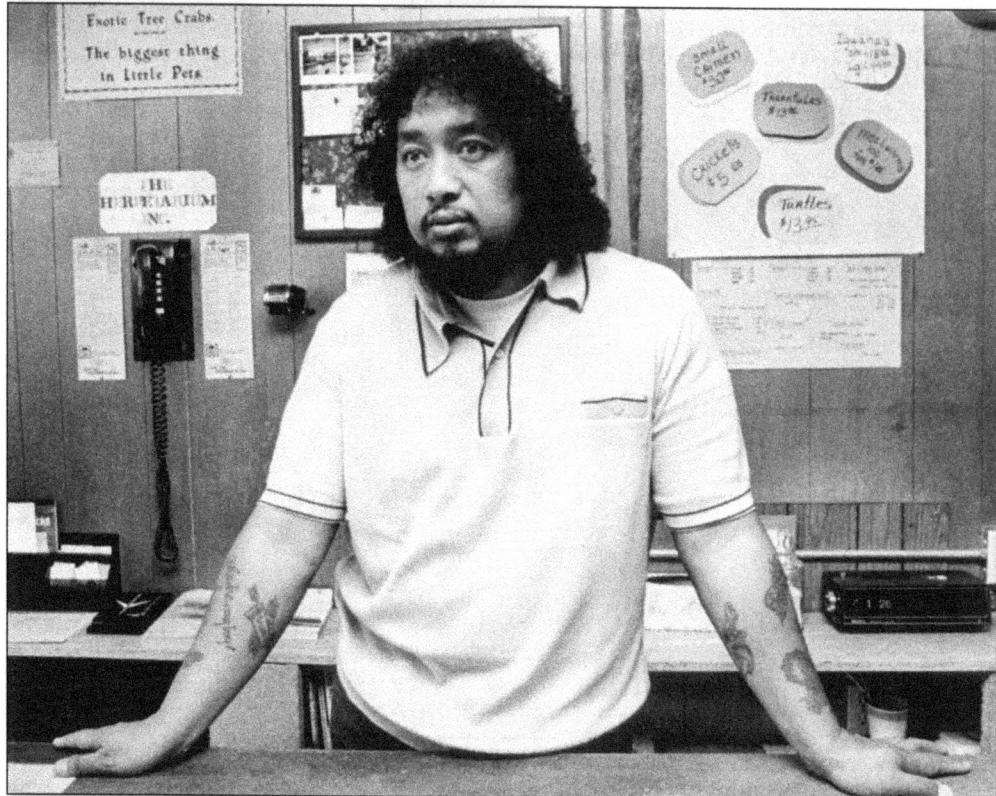

Filipinos have owned all types of businesses in Vallejo. One of the most unusual was the Herpetarium owned by Tom Quenga. His reptile store was located on Benicia Road in 1980. He brought his snakes to schools and other events, teaching people about them and their upkeep. He had a fascination with snakes ever since he was a kid growing up in South Vallejo, much to the chagrin of his mother. (Courtesy of *Vallejo Times-Herald*.)

Tony Magsanay was the manager of the City Hall Shell Station at the corner of Capitol and Marin Streets in 1961. The gas station was one of the busiest in town because it was next to the city hall and across the street from the Federal Building. Today it is a parking lot for the museum and a mortuary. (Courtesy of *Vallejo Times-Herald*.)

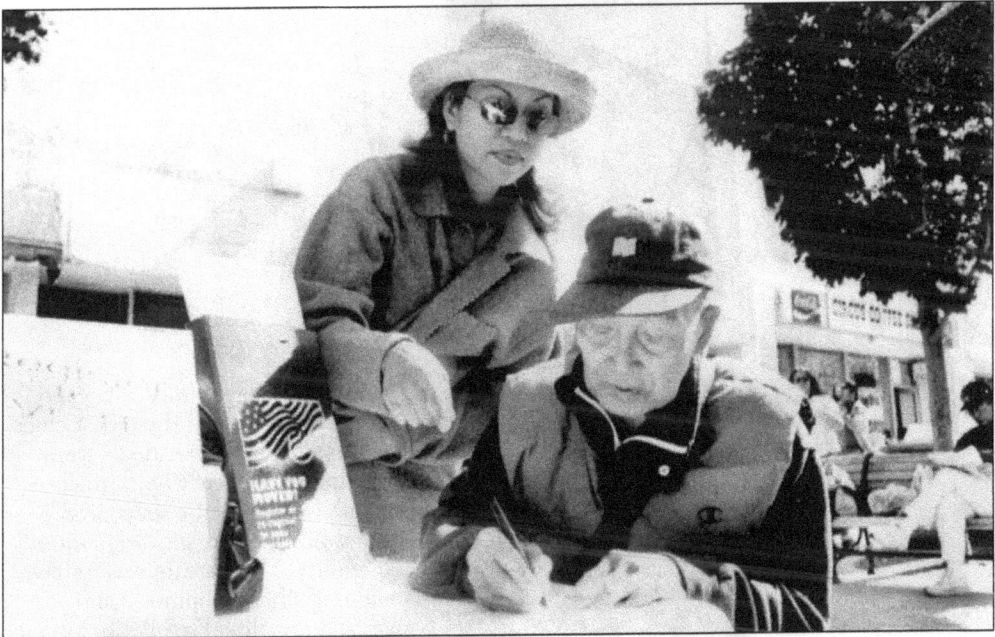

Registering Filipinos to vote has been a major undertaking of the Filipino-American Democratic Club of Vallejo. The weekly Saturday morning farmer's market on Georgia Street is a prime location to register voters. Filipino voters, especially senior citizens and veterans, help build the community's political clout. Belle Orpilla, a member of the club, assists a senior citizen with filling out a voter registration form in 2002. (Courtesy of Mel Orpilla.)

Filipino medical professionals began coming to America after the Immigration and Nationality Act of 1965. Initially, more than half of those immigrating were Filipina nurses. Every medical clinic, health center, nursing facility, and hospital, has Filipino staff. This group of Kaiser Permanente Hospital employees are, from left to right, Elaine Dominguez, Michelle Labon, Grace Prado, Imelda Olmedo, Nora Flores, Agnes Solla, and Ed Dumaguin (seated). (Courtesy of Ed Dumaguin.)

The Filipino Community of Solano County, Inc. is one of the oldest clubs in Vallejo. Its early presidents were the Filipino pioneers who formed the club to address the social and cultural needs of the growing Filipino community. Their dream was to have a building where Filipinos could meet and socialize. Fred Pono, former president of the club, carried on those ideals and became the visionary behind Vallejo's Philippine Cultural Month. He is pictured here c. 1992. (Courtesy of Mel Orpilla.)

In the 1980s, Springs Road in East Vallejo was becoming a mecca for Filipino-owned businesses. These included real estate, insurance, CPAs, a veterinarian, and restaurants and markets. Today it serves the large Filipino population on the east side of Interstate 80. Andrea Foods, located at 1109 Maple Avenue at the corner of Springs Road, is regarded as one of the best Filipino restaurants in the Bay Area. (Courtesy of Mel Orpilla.)

A Vallejo Filipino landmark, the Kajukenbo Self-Defense Institute, is the oldest, continuously operated Filipino-owned business in Vallejo. Generations of families have learned Kajukenbo, a martial art developed in Hawaii by Filipino-American professor Adriano Emperado. Grandmaster Emil Bautista has taught in his building at 974 Benicia Road since 1968. The building was formerly a five and dime store, then a television repair store. It also serves as a Filipino martial arts center and history museum of Vallejo martial artists. (Courtesy of Mel Orpilla.)

Crisostomo Villanueva was a candidate for City Council in 1987. He won in 1990, becoming the second Filipino to sit on the City Council since Larry Asera in 1976, and served two distinguished terms. He is an accountant by profession with an accounting firm in Vallejo. He continues to stay active in local politics and community organizations. (Courtesy of *Vallejo Times Herald*.)

In 2001, the Filipino-American Educators Association of CA–North Bay Chapter, honored Linda Alemania for being the first Filipino teacher hired in the Vallejo School District. Pictured, from left to right, are Linda Alemania, Rozzana Verder-Aliga of the Vallejo City Unified School District Board, and Larry Asera, Solano County Board of Education. The schools in Vallejo have hired a large number of Filipino teachers and administrators under the leadership of Rozzana and Larry. (Courtesy of Mel Orpilla.)

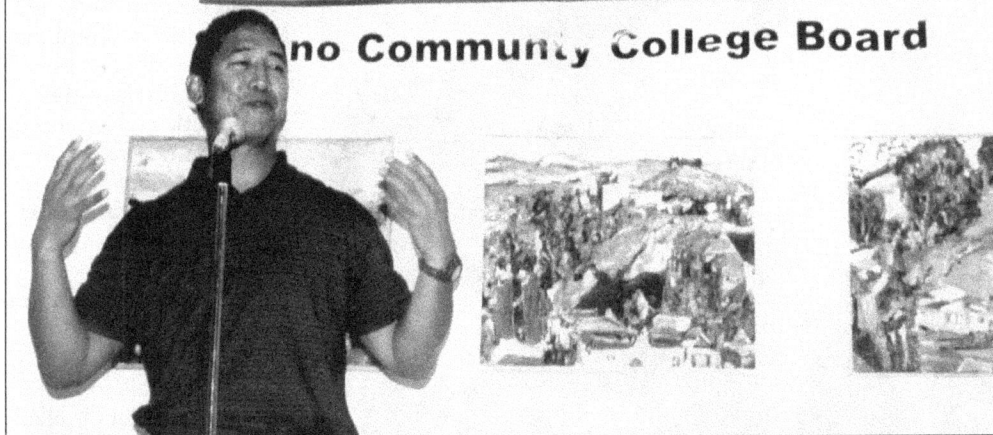

MEL ORPILLA

...no Community College Board

In 2002, author Mel Orpilla campaigned for a seat on the Solano Community College Board. Filipinos represent the largest group of "students of color" at Solano College. Mel was a former student at the college, as was his son Jacob, sister Luella, and his mother, Ofelia. In 2002, Filipinos accounted for at least 16 percent of the enrollment, yet had never had a Filipino college board member represent their interests. Although he lost, there will no doubt be efforts by members of the Filipino community in the future. (Courtesy of Belle Orpilla.)

Filipino teachers in the school district like Nieves Fernandez have made great contributions to their students' educational goals. Nieves (on right, wearing hat and dark glasses), a Franklin Middle School teacher, worked with special education students. She came to America as a college student and was married to the late Victor Fernandez, a "Manong," and former member of the First Filipino Batallion, c. 2000. (Courtesy Nieves Fernandez.)

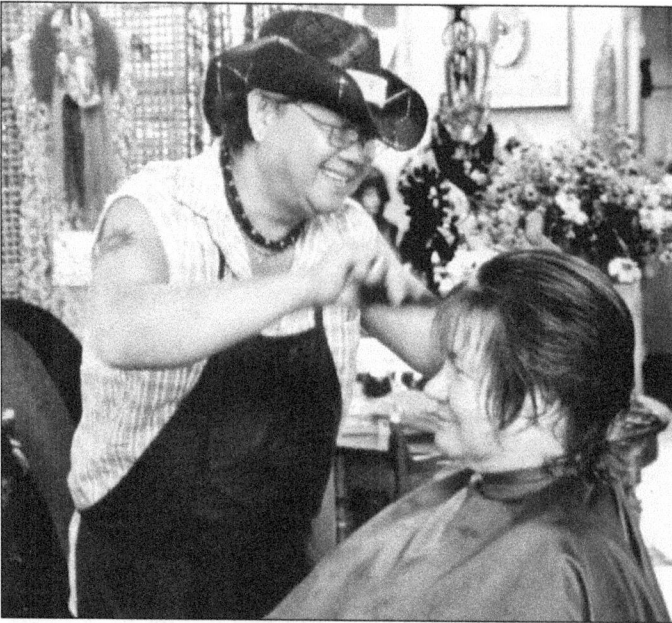

"Adolfo" is one of the most popular hairstylists in Vallejo. His art-themed Adolfo Hair Studio at 721 Marin Street in downtown Vallejo also doubles as a gallery for his paintings and eclectic collections. He is shown here cutting the hair of Mary Fraser. Adolfo is one of the most creative people in Vallejo. He paints, dances, and designs clothes in addition to styling hair. Filipino beauty salons abound throughout Vallejo. (Courtesy of Mel Orpilla.)

In 1995, the popular television show *Frasier* stated that Filipina women were available as "mail order brides." The Filipino community responded to this unfair representation by holding a rally on the steps of city hall on Santa Clara Street. Young and old participated. Pastor Tony Ubalde, Fellowship United Methodist Church, lead the rally as members of the audience held up signs. Filipinos in Vallejo are no longer a passive community. As this rally illustrates, they let their opinions be known to all. (Courtesy of Mel Orpilla.)

Originally planned for the corner of Grant and Cherry Streets a few blocks away, the leaders of the Filipino Community bought this building in the 1950s instead. The Filipino Community Center is located at 820 Sonoma Boulevard, and was formerly a laundry. Many organizations and families rent the building to hold meetings and parties. It underwent a massive remodeling in the late 1990s and is now another Vallejo Filipino landmark whose interior walls are lined with photos of past presidents and queen contest winners spanning more than 50 years. (Courtesy of Mel Orpilla.)

Roger Chan, Rev. Emeliano Valle, and Jose Altson pray for peace at the Filipino Community Center in 1986. The city had just suffered through a rash of violence affecting Filipinos. Filipinos have always turned to prayer in trying times. Organized prayer groups proliferate around Vallejo and provide a religious as well as social outlet for many Filipinos, a tradition brought from the Philippines. Vallejo is home to numerous Filipino-based churches, including two Filipino Baptist churches, United Church of Christ, Inglesia ni Cristo, Church of the Nazarene, United Methodist, and over a dozen others. Catholicism is still the dominant religion amongst Filipinos. (Courtesy of *Vallejo Times-Herald*.)

When he arrived in America in 1926 and came to Vallejo in the 1930s, Nazario Orpilla never dreamed that he would witness the closing of Mare Island Naval Shipyard, which was founded in 1853. Vallejo was a company town with Mare Island as the major employer. From the first Filipinos brought to Mare Island after the end of the Spanish American War to the laborers and craftsmen and women in the mid-20th century and finally to the medical professionals and skilled employees at its closing in 1996, Mare Island was at the heart of the Filipino presence in Vallejo. Nazario worked there for 37 years, retiring in 1974. He is the patriarch of the Orpilla family now, five generations deep and is shown here at Mare Island Naval Shipyard where he first worked in 1932. In October 2004 he returned to Mare Island for the first time since he retired in 1974. (Courtesy of Mel Orpilla.)

In this 1996 photo, Robert and Lavella Mangoba Wilson kiss their one-year-old son, Kaleo, a fourth-generation Filipino Vallejoan and the great-grandson of Nazario Orpilla. Kaleo represents the future of Filipinos in Vallejo, where the population was approximately 25,000 in 2000. Almost one in four people in Vallejo are Filipino and represent all sectors of the community while continuing to contribute to the social, economic, and political vibrancy of the city. (Courtesy of Mel Orpilla.)

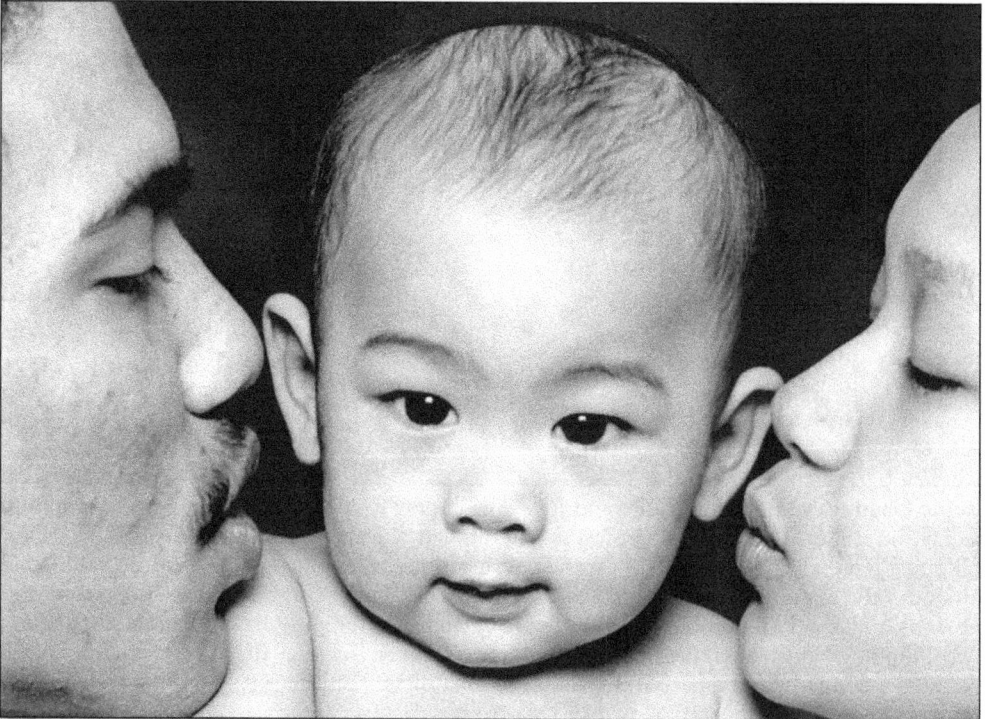